National Trust

— COMPLETE —

Pies, Stews & One-Pot Meals

Laura Mason

National Trust

— COMPLETE —

Pies, Stews & One-Pot Meals

Laura Mason

National Trust

First published in the United Kingdom in 2011

This edition published in 2014 by
National Trust Books, an imprint of Pavilion Books Company Ltd
1 Gower Street
London WC1E 6HD
www.pavilionbooks.com

ISBN: 9781909881327

A CIP catalogue record for this book is available from the
British Library.

20 19 18 17 16 15 14
10 9 8 7 6 5 4 3 2 1

Reproduction by Mission Productions Ltd, Hong Kong
Printed and bound by Toppan Leefung Printing Ltd, China

Design by Rosamund Saunders
Food photography by Tara Fisher
Home economy by Jane Suthering
Styling by Wei Tang

For more information on game contact Game-to-Eat, The Countryside
Alliance Foundation's campaign dedicated to increasing the eating and
enjoyment of British wild game. Visit www.gametoeat.co.uk for more
information.

This book can be ordered direct from the publisher at the website:
www.pavilionbooks.com, or try your local bookshop. Also available at
National Trust shops or www.shop.nationaltrust.org.uk.

Contents

Introduction

STEWS, PIES AND ROASTS ARE COMFORTING DISHES. A hearty beef pie or a meat stew with dumplings or mashed potato suits raw days. Just the smell of it cooking lifts the hearts of those who are feeling low, weary or cold, or just plain hungry. These dishes use inexpensive cuts of meat and are economical of fuel using one pot. What's more, they can be prepared and left in a low oven while the cook does something else, or be reheated at a later date. These are quiet and good-tempered dishes.

Both stews and pies are also much more varied than mere chunks of meat and onions in a thick brown gravy. They belong to traditional British cookery, but I have explored other possibilities: unthickened sauces that are light and fresh; a large piece of meat instead of cubes; pies served cold instead of hot. There are also recipes for fish and vegetable stews and pies.

Think of a roast and we visualise vast joints of beef turning on spits in front of huge fires, of venison poached from under the gamekeeper's nose, of medieval boards groaning under the weight of peacocks, swans and sucking pigs, of Christmas geese and turkeys, and of convivial Sunday dinners. In short, a roast is an idea of plenty, of feasting (legitimate or otherwise), and of occasion. Over the years this has been allowed to decline into the bland reality of gravy granules and ready meals.

The idea of the stew

A stew is a dish composed with an end result in mind. In the 18th century, the term for them was 'made dishes'. Fricassée, jug, haricot, civet, ragoût, daube, braise, fricandeau, carbonnade, hot pot, casserole, blanquette – many of our ideas about stews date from the Georgian period of this time, often derived from French cookery. Fricassées were slices of meat cooked in a liquid thickened by egg yolks beaten with lemon juice or white wine. Over time, the mixture lost the acid and was instead thickened by cream or a roux, so now it's associated with a creamy sauce. Haricot, civet and daube also had specific meanings: 'haricot' denoted something cut into pieces; 'civet' derived from a word for onions; and 'daube' referred to a method used for cooking in a pot with aromatics and wine or vinegar. Ragoûts, or 'ragoos', were made from extracts of beef, veal, ham or partridge, and tasty morsels poured around joints of meat, whole fish or vegetables.

Some names imply a particular cooking dish. The French donated the word 'casserole', which in the 18th century meant a rice border moulded into the shape of a cooking pot, and holding a savoury mixture. By the late 19th century, it indicated meat and vegetable dishes in closed pots cooked slowly in the oven. Both the pot and the contents became known as casseroles. The notion of the container links stews to pies. One type of pie was made with a pastry of coarse flour, water and a little fat. The pastry was inedible and was set by baking, which also cooked the contents – meat, poultry or game. Other pies had fillings more akin to a stew but, eventually, the lower crust vanished, leaving the type of pie that is still part of our culinary landscape.

The idea of the roast

Good meat for a roast is expensive and, to some extent, a luxury. This is how it should be – as, too, should be the ability to use meat left over from one meal to make another, equally appealing meal. Meat is a resource that is likely to become scarcer – and well-produced meat even more so. We should value it properly for what it is – a food in which months, or possibly years, of an animal's life is concentrated into a package of protein and fat. An element of a long-held idea that British meat is so good that it needs no 'messing about' still persists, but before the 19th century strong flavours were appreciated, as they are once again. Many of the recipes given here try to capture some of the flavours of the past, using as inspiration recipes from historic cookery texts that would undoubtedly have found their way into the kitchens of houses now owned by the National Trust. Also included are a few forays into current fashions.

A roast forms a special part of British eating habits, even if it is not quite the weekly punctuation mark it once was. Changes in taste and lifestyle have influenced how we eat; but a well-chosen piece of meat, carefully cooked, is an opportunity for conviviality, a gathering of family and friends. Originally, roasting meant cooking by exposing meat to radiant heat in front of an open fire. Even casual inspection of historic cookery books shows that this was considered an important method for cooking meat (and to a lesser extent, fish). Foreigners remarked on English skill in roasting.

Spit-roast meat didn't taste of smoke: it cooked in front of the fire, not over it. Fat dripped into a pan set below, with no possibility of overheating. Trying to re-create the flavour of the past is difficult, but experiments give excellent results: succulent, cleanly flavoured, with crisp coatings. Managing the fire correctly, knowing how to spit a joint so that the weight was evenly distributed around it and how close to put the meat to the fire were all special skills. As a cook, one had to know how to prepare, or dress, and present all sorts of roasts; as a guest, to be able to carve was a desirable social skill. Leftovers were expected and were part of the domestic economy of large households.

A major difference between then and now is we cook meat in an oven. Technically, this is baking, but it is now the accepted roasting method. The change to oven roasting began after the coal-fired kitchen range was invented in the 1790s; gas and electric ovens followed in the 19th century. To people accustomed to spit-roast meat, the change was significant and not for the better. In an oven, meat effectively fries in the hot fat that drips from it, and escaping juices make the fat spit, splashing on the sides of the tin, where it burns. The texture of oven-cooked roasts is also different: closer and drier.

Seasonings and accompaniments for roasts have changed over the centuries, from medieval combinations of spices, through tastes for citrus and anchovies, and rich meaty concoctions to the 'plain cookery' of the late 19th century; our adoption of Mediterranean and Asian flavours is another link in this chain. Some items that have shown remarkable persistence are bread sauce, mustard, apple sauce, sage and onion, and redcurrant jelly, all established in the way that we use them today by the 18th century. We look for potatoes to accompany our roasts, but until the end of that century our ancestors would have expected pudding, perhaps a spherical, breadcrumb-and-flour plum one, or a batter type, still with us as Yorkshire pudding.

Cooking Pies and Stews

Making a basic stew is all about harmonising ingredients and developing flavours – this means allowing tougher cuts of meat to become tender and blending them with a selection of root vegetables and flavourings into a well-seasoned and pleasing entity.

Choosing a container

Most people acquire a casserole that becomes a favourite because it cooks food well, holds the right amount for the family's needs and looks good. For the past 20 years, a round cast-iron Le Creuset casserole, enamelled in classic flame orange, has been my favourite. If nothing else is available, a large, reasonably heavy pan or deep frying pan will hold a stew for simmering over a low flame (alternatively, it can be put in the oven if it is designed for this, but do remember that the handle will get very hot). Lids for any stewing pan or pot should be close-fitting, although it's always possible to improvise with tinfoil.

Casseroles exist in colourful diversity, and it is nice to have one that looks good at the table. One that can be used both on the hob and in the oven is useful. This generally means stainless or enamelled steel, enamelled cast iron or tinned copper. Cast-iron pots are heavy and expensive to buy, but with care they last for decades. They come in cheerful colours and retain heat well. Try not to drop them, especially on stone floors: cast iron is brittle and enamel chips. Their surfaces also need to be treated with care. Soak to remove any food that is burnt on, and avoid harsh abrasives. Cast iron without enamelling can be used, but any acid ingredients will react with the metal. This is not life-threatening, but it does give the sauce a strange colour. Steel, copper, or combinations of both make durable cooking pots. They are easy to care for unless completely made of copper, in which case the tin lining must be maintained (these are the traditional choice in professional kitchens).

Toughened glass and many ceramic casseroles are inexpensive and durable, and come in designs to suit all tastes and styles of decoration, but they normally can't be used on the hob. Here, a frying pan will be needed for operations requiring direct heat (such as sweating or frying and bringing sauces to the boil), and these ingredients must then be added to the casserole when it is ready to go in the oven. This is not necessarily a disadvantage, but it does mean more washing-up. Of traditional ceramics, stoneware is the most hard wearing. Very rustic earthenware pots (the sort sometimes brought back from Mediterranean holidays) look wonderful and can be used, but they may be better as ornaments: they are often not very durable and are easily chipped, with glazes that tend to be porous or which will craze and so eventually become difficult to clean. Such pots belong to cultures where the slow heat of embers on the hearth or a cooling bread oven are not entirely forgotten, and replacements can be easily and cheaply acquired.

Pie dishes are widely available. The deep-filled pies given in the following recipes require round, oblong or oval pie dishes. They should have wide rims to support the edges of the pastry covering (unless using individual pie dishes of the sort used in pubs, which rarely do). Pie dishes are widely available in earthenware, glass or enamelled iron and share the various advantages and disadvantages of these materials. Traditional English pie funnels shaped as blackbirds are a nice traditional touch to support the pastry in the centre and allow steam to escape.

Meat

Many different recipes for stews exist, but there is a general method for English brown stews, varying only according to taste and the contents of the larder. The method applies principally to meat; fish and vegetables need different management. Choose a cut of meat that is appropriate (see individual recipes for suggestions) and cut it into suitable pieces. Cubes that are roughly 2.5cm (1in) along each side are usually suggested, but the pieces can be up to twice as big, especially for venison and beef stews. For larger pieces, the cooking time may be a little longer. Steaks and chops can be stewed without further dividing (meat isn't usually cut into strips). Remove any obvious bits of gristle or large pieces of fat. Use kitchen paper to pat the meat dry. For many stews, the meat must first be fried, and wet meat doesn't brown as easily. Dredging the meat with flour before frying also helps to absorb moisture and will thicken the sauce as it cooks.

Marinating is often suggested for meat for stews, especially wine-based marinades. This has little effect on the texture of meat, but is an excellent method for flavouring it. Drain the meat well before cooking and reserve the marinade for the sauce, unless otherwise instructed.

Bacon, or its Italian equivalent, pancetta, should be unsmoked. These provide both fat and flavour for stews. Pancetta can be bought in lardons or cubes, or ask for a thick slice from a delicatessen and cut it up at home. It is usually fairly fatty. Choose bacon carefully, looking for a dry cure with quite a lot of fat. Bacon tends to be ready-cut into rashers, which are fine for cutting into matchsticks. For cubes, though, you will need to acquire a whole piece and cut it yourself.

Frying

Frying is not an essential step in making a stew – some, including Irish Stew, don't call for it at all – but as a general rule it is a good idea. Browning the meat adds depth of flavour, although it does absolutely nothing to retain the juices, whatever the culinary old wives say. If starting with bacon or pancetta, allow it to cook until most of the fat has been yielded and it is starting to crisp. Remove the pieces with a slotted spoon and keep to one side while frying the other ingredients in the fat. If necessary, add extra fat to the chosen casserole, or a frying pan if the former isn't flameproof, and allow it to get reasonably hot for frying other ingredients.

Vegetables such as chopped onions are usually fried first to help develop flavour. Fairly high heat and frequent stirring speed things along, but don't let the vegetables burn. Timings given for frying vary enormously across recipes but are usually in the range of 'a few minutes'. Such advice is not especially helpful. Over the years I've come to prefer frying vegetables until quite well cooked. Choose between leaving them on a low heat, checking occasionally and turning to make sure they cook evenly; or turning up the heat, frying briskly and turning frequently until they begin to develop golden-brown patches. Watch how they are cooking, and aim for a state in which they have lost some water and the natural sugars they contain have begun to caramelise: the pieces will shrink and start to look golden, especially the onions. If they are allowed to go much darker, they will start to burn. Remove them from the pot with a slotted spoon, allowing as much fat as possible to drain. Use this to fry the meat, in batches if necessary, turning so that the pieces are browned on all sides.

Additional fat is often needed. Most people have their own tastes; I prefer butter but beef dripping and lard are traditional choices for meaty stews; goose and duck fat are fashionable; olive oil and other vegetable fats are considered healthier. Avoid lamb and mutton fat; they are strongly flavoured and cling to the palate. The recipes suggest what I consider to be minimum amounts, and more may make for easier cooking. Excess fat can always be removed from the surface of a stew at the end.

Vegetables and seasonings

The base of fried vegetables depends to some extent on the nature of the stew. Onions are routinely used for an English stew. Garlic, celery, carrot or turnip are sometimes added (but avoid leeks, which develop an unpleasant taste and texture when fried). These should be chopped evenly and fairly finely, unless otherwise directed. Ordinary cultivated mushrooms are another frequent addition. Button ones are often left whole, but I prefer to slice any mushrooms and fry until the slices are starting to turn golden. They will soak up whatever fat is in the pan initially; as they cook, the liquid they contain starts to evaporate and they give some of the fat back again.

Seasoning is a matter for individual taste. Salt is the most basic addition; be a little on the mean side when adding it at the start of cooking, and remember that stock cubes and some flavourings such as soy sauce are salty. Always taste a finished stew before adding any more. Once the salt has been added, it is almost impossible to remove. A method sometimes quoted for rescuing a stew that has been over-salted is to peel several large potatoes and put them into the stew to cook. Remove them when done, and they will have absorbed some of the salt. Provided the amount of salt is not vastly overdone, this can be quite effective, but it is better not to add too much salt in the first place.

Pepper is next on the list, almost as ubiquitous as salt for seasoning savoury dishes. Use freshly ground black pepper. Again, amounts are difficult to specify: add and taste until the dish is right for you. Some people like to use combinations of peppercorns – black for aroma, white for heat, green for a mild piquancy, allspice for a slightly perfumed note. Allspice – or Jamaica pepper, as 18th-century cooks called it – is unrelated to pepper but makes a good seasoning for red meats. Of other spices,

a pinch of cayenne or chilli powder wakes up the palate and is especially good in dishes with turkey, wild duck and hare. Nutmeg and mace are both good in meat dishes, as 18th-century cooks knew when assembling meaty ragoos and braised dishes. Buy nutmeg whole and grate, or pound the long yellow-orange blades of mace with a pestle and mortar as needed. Parsley finds its way into many dishes, as a seasoning and a garnish. Chop finely and add just after the liquid when cooking, or scatter over a finished stew for fresh colour and added flavour. Thyme and marjoram are good in many stews, and lemon thyme is delicious in veal and fish dishes – strip the leaves off the stems before using. Tarragon is good with chicken and rabbit; use rosemary sparingly.

Recipes often call for a bouquet garni, the little bunch of herbs dropped into a stew after the liquid is added and removed just before the end of cooking. These generally include parsley, a bay leaf, some thyme and other herbs according to the recipe, perhaps with a piece of lemon or orange zest, tied up with thin string or thread. Or use the green leaf of a leek, well washed, to enclose something a little more elaborate: lay a piece of leaf flat, put the herbs and some black peppercorns plus any other desired spices on it, fold the leaf to enclose them and tie up like a parcel. Retrieve and discard a bouquet garni from the sauce before serving a stew.

Some herbs have to be grown – notably chervil, which is difficult to buy; and summer or winter savory, which are both highly aromatic and a little like thyme, but which seem difficult to obtain as cut herbs. Dried herbs are useful, though some dry better than others. Bay, rosemary, thyme and marjoram lose least in terms of perfume. One teaspoon of dried herb is equivalent to about 1 tablespoon of the same freshly chopped, so when adding to dishes treat with respect.

Mushroom products are also useful for seasoning, following the habits of 250 years ago. Field mushrooms were made into strongly flavoured ketchup, a version of which is still available – try adding a little to a beef or game stew. Soak dried porcini mushrooms to add savour to meat stews or make a good vegetarian stock. Italian delicatessens sell various truffle and porcini pastes in jars.

Adding liquids

Water is the most basic cooking medium and can be used in default of other cooking liquids. A well-made stock adds depth of flavour and even a simple one made by simmering a carrot and onion with the bones from a Sunday chicken or a rib of beef will help a stew along. If time and resources allow, make a more complex one using bones from meat appropriate to the recipe. Strong, well-reduced beef stock was essential in the French-influenced cookery of England in the 18th and early 19th centuries, and was added to all kinds of dishes, probably giving a similar flavour. Stock cubes tend to share this disadvantage, but are adequate if nothing else is available. Commercially produced stocks have become available in other forms – in plastic pouches, jars or as heavily reduced pastes – and are good alternatives to home-made ones.

Wine is frequently used in stews and casseroles. The usual basic rule applies: if you wouldn't drink it, then don't cook with it. This doesn't mean choosing a fine vintage wine, but do always use a good wine, and not the end of a bottle that has lingered in a warm kitchen until it has turned to vinegar. It should always be added at an early stage of cooking for the flavour to mellow. Wine usually makes a good marinade. Fortified wines, especially port and Madeira, are often used with game.

Beer, likewise, is a good addition to many stews, especially those made with beef or game such as venison. Like wine, it can be used as a marinade and needs to be cooked for a long time to get the best out of the flavour. Recent fashions in brewing have tended towards strongly hopped brews – these should be avoided for cooking because they make stews cooked with them unpalatably bitter. Look for traditionally English mild, bitter or brown ale; winter ales, with a higher alcohol content and slight sweetness, can also be good. Cider is another traditional product that is sometimes added to stews. Use a well-made variety and allow it long cooking to mellow the flavour. It is often chosen as a cooking liquid for rabbit, pork and, to a lesser extent, chicken.

Juices and other fruit-based products also play a role. Apple juice provides a sweeter, less assertive alternative to cider; add some lemon juice if it tastes too sweet. Another possibility is verjuice, the juice of unripe grapes or apples. Formerly, this was prepared in every large kitchen in the country, but it went out of use sometime around the end of the 17th century. It has been revived by a few winemakers and can be bought bottled and pasteurised from good delicatessens. Less aggressive in flavour than vinegar and more complex than lemon juice, it adds a gentle fruity acidity to sauces.

Lemon juice adds a slightly acid note to any recipe requiring it. Orange juice has a more dominant flavour, but lifts stews made with red meat and is a good flavouring for liver. Redcurrant jelly is a traditional way of adding a sweet-sour fruitiness to game stews, but other fruit jellies are available – try quince, plum or damson. In the past, recipes calling for vinegar had the British cook reaching for a bottle of dark brown malt vinegar. These days, it is considered to have an aggressive flavour, although it was often used in dishes of braised steak, and a little can be added towards the end of cooking in beer-based stews. Wine or cider vinegars add acidity without the underlying maltiness, but in recent years balsamic vinegar has swept all before it. Traditionally made aged balsamic vinegar from Modena in northern Italy is expensive and far too precious to be added to stews, but cheaper versions add a sour-sweet, caramel flavour.

Thickening

A common method for thickening stews is essentially based on the idea of a roux. For beef stews, flour is added at the start, often used to toss the meat, or shaken into the fat left over from frying. Liquid is added to make the sauce and the mixture cooks down to thicken the gravy. This is a method best used with stews cooked in the oven, because it has a tendency to stick to the base of the pan when used on direct heat – either add enough liquid to make the sauce quite thin at the start, or keep stirring and top up if necessary.

Stews cooked without added flour are often thickened at the end. *Beurre manié* is one option; this consists of equal quantities of butter and flour worked together to a paste. When cooking is complete, uncover the stew and dot the mixture over the surface in small pieces. Shake the pan to absorb it, or stir gently. The butter should melt into the mixture, distributing the flour to thicken it. Once again, do not allow the dish to boil again or be tempted to reheat it. Using about 30g (1oz) of plain flour and 30g (1oz) of butter is ample for thickening a stew for four people.

Adding arrowroot or cornflour is a simple way of thickening sauces; arrowroot produces a finer result. Put the arrowroot or cornflour in a cup or small bowl and add a little cold water, mixing to obtain a smooth thin paste. Pour this into the hot (not boiling) stew and stir to distribute evenly. Heat gently to bring the mixture to the boil and thicken it. It should take only a couple of minutes to do this. The flavour is neutral and there are no problems about reheating dishes thickened this way, although prolonged heat may affect the starch and thin the sauce a little.

For stews based on pale meats, fish or vegetables, an egg yolk mixture can be used, as in a fricassée. Beat the yolks together with the lemon juice, wine, vinegar or cream. Remove the dish from the heat and allow it to cool a little, then stir in the mixture. It should thicken the sauce lightly – you may also need to reheat it carefully to encourage this, but avoid too much heat, or the egg will cook and curdle the sauce. Don't allow it to boil again. Three egg yolks and about 100ml (3½fl oz) of the liquid ingredient will thicken a stew for four people. This method has a significant effect on flavour (and colour if cream is added), and should not be used with stews intended for reheating.

Some ingredients for stews act naturally as thickeners. Potatoes often start to break down in the sauce and some people positively encourage this, stirring to help it along, because they like the texture. Very well-made stocks, especially veal-based ones, are gelatinous and gain body as the liquid evaporates. In the past, their flavour, texture and transparency were valued for adding to rich stews of all descriptions; cooks made and kept supplies of well-reduced veal stock, which they called glaze. This does require making stock yourself, but if you discover a meat stew is on the liquid side at the end of cooking, try ladling some of the broth into a separate pan and boiling hard to reduce it. This concentrates the flavour (so don't season until the end) and also adds a little more body to the stock. A little butter added right at the end of cooking also adds flavour and gloss – but don't reheat, or it will separate out.

Times and temperatures

One of the best things about stews is their flexibility. Combine the ingredients, pour into a casserole, cover and put in a low oven. If the pot seems to need an extra seal, put a layer of tinfoil or a double sheet of greaseproof paper, trimmed to fit, under the lid. Leave well alone for 2–3 hours. At the end of this time, the result should be a perfectly good stew; put it back for a bit longer if it's not quite done. The gentle heat of the bottom oven of an Aga is ideal. If you are not cooking to a deadline and can review progress occasionally, that is really all you need to do.

However, I have suggested times and temperatures in the recipes. A slow oven means anything from as low as the oven allows through 140–150°C, 275–300°F, Gas mark 1–2. Times will be a little more or a little less depending on how accurate the thermostat is. The tougher the meat, the longer and slower cooking should be. Higher temperatures – say, a moderate oven of 180°C, 350°F, Gas mark 4 – are fine with meat that is already fairly tender, such as poultry or young game birds. Cooking times are quicker, say between 1 hour and 1½ hours, for chicken portions. Pies need a different approach, as the pastry needs to set – and to rise, if using puff pastry (see page 25).

Cooking stews on the hob is probably less easy for us than it was in the past. To do this well, the liquid needs to be kept just below boiling – only the slightest movement should be apparent on the surface. The simmering plate of an Aga does very well, but neither gas nor electricity seem capable of the really low heat needed. Nor have I ever had much success with the various mats sold to put under pans to distribute low heat evenly across the base – but if they work for you, then that is an option. Slow cookers can also be used for cooking stews, and need even less attention. Follow the manufacturer's instructions for heating them and in relation to settings for different types of meat.

Removing fat
A cooked meat stew often has a fair amount of excess fat on the surface, either from frying the ingredients in the initial stages or from fat that is given up by the meat during the cooking process. If serving the stew immediately, remove as much fat as possible by skimming it off with a spoon or blotting the surface with kitchen paper, trying not to pick up any of the sauce in the process. Otherwise, allow the stew to cool and then chill in the fridge overnight. The next day, it is easy to lift the solidified fat off the surface.

Reheating
With the exception of stews that are made from veal or game birds (in which the meat tends to dryness), most meat stews taste better after reheating the next day, when the flavours have had a chance to mellow and blend. This offers the convenience of being able to make a complex dish the day before it is needed – or the week or month before if stored in the freezer. Store cooled stews in a cold larder or the fridge overnight, or pour into a suitable container for freezing. Leave any final thickenings or additions such as breadcrumbs or dumplings until you are ready to reheat a stew. Those based on vegetables or fish don't reheat well, as the fresh flavours and subtle textures are lost in the process.

A frozen stew is best defrosted for several hours before needed. Don't worry too much if the sauce appears to separate; it should come back together with a little stirring when the mixture is hot again. For reheating, put the mixture into a suitable serving dish. Heat in a moderate oven at 180°C, 350°F, Gas mark 4 for about 30 minutes or until the mixture is, in that old-fashioned lovely English phrase, 'piping hot' – in other words, not far off boiling. Stir it from time to time. If you prefer, reheat the stew gently in a pan, but watch carefully and stir frequently to make sure the mixture heats evenly and doesn't stick to the pan. A little water can be added to thin particularly thick sauces during the process if desired. You can add any finishing touches, such as dumplings or bread-based toppings, as the stew is reheated.

Cooking Roasts
The first rule of good roasting is to buy good meat. The British Isles have long been recognised for producing excellent meat, especially beef and mutton, but many factors other than simply 'buying British' come under consideration – flavour, price, animal welfare and place of origin. A roast from a supermarket can produce a reasonable meal, but one from a butcher or sourced

directly from a farmer is likely to give something much better. Some suppliers are expensive, but others may be cheaper than supermarkets, and a knowledgeable supplier can tell you more about the animals. Meat lies at the end of the food chain and represents a concentrated and precious food resource. The idea that it should be cheap is erroneous, and on balance it is better to pay a bit more for something well produced and to eat a bit less.

Intensive systems do not automatically equate with poor animal welfare, but for excellent flavour, a traditional slow-growing animal is likely to provide better meat. Animal welfare systems have been the subject of much debate over the past 30 years, and several assurance schemes exist to provide the consumer with some idea of how the food on their plate has been produced. There are four principal schemes, all voluntary, and each with a slightly different emphasis: Assured Food Standards ('Red Tractor'); RSPCA Freedom Food (this is the minimum welfare standard that the National Trust will accept from its tenant farmers and when sourcing meat for its restaurants); LEAF (Linking the Environment and Farming); and Soil Association.

Most domestic animals and birds are from commercial stock bred for specific characteristics. Flavour is rarely top of the list – though leanness, fast growth, small bone structure and esoteric factors such as 'double-muscling' may be. Traditional British breeds of cattle, sheep and pig tend to be smaller, slower growing and have more capacity to gain fat than continental breeds, but slow growth can provide tastier meat, and distinctive appearance adds diversity to the landscape. Some breeds are considered 'rare', existing in limited numbers. There are several marketing schemes for their meat and, while eating something rare may seem odd, increasing demand for their meat helps ensure survival.

In conventional agriculture, maximum growth in minimum time is achieved partly by using specially bred animals. They tend to be reared on commercially produced concentrates made from a range of by-products whose composition depends on price. This applies especially to pigs and poultry, whose flesh can be dull and bland. It is less of an issue with beef, which is at least partially grass fed, and least of all with sheep, who graze pasture, moorland or saltmarsh. Farmers who take an interest in flavour often try to grow at least some of their own grain and other fodder crops for poultry, pigs and cattle. Feeding makes most difference to pigs and poultry, and as a general rule, any animal which has roamed freely will be more interesting on the plate.

Don't forget that meat, especially from cattle and sheep, has a strong link with our treasured landscape. Rainfall, temperature and topography are all well suited to grassland, and often quite large areas that are unsuitable for growing crops will sustain cattle and sheep. The landscape includes many areas of distinctive flora, often partially created by grazing animals, including cattle grazed on the rich lowland pastures of the Somerset Levels or the sweet grasses of the limestone uplands of West Yorkshire, or mutton from the Lake District fells or the short turf of the South Downs.

The age at which an animal is killed for meat also influences flavour. Most farmers don't want their stock lounging in field or shed eating expensive food after they have reached the optimum weight, so the majority comes from relatively young animals: lamb will be on the market at 4–5 months old, a pig at just under 4 months. The BSE epidemic led to restrictions on the age at which beef cattle could be sold for meat, but they are now allowed to grow up to the age of 48 months (although the majority become meat at 30 months). Cattle breeds traditional to Britain score well for flavour, but take a long time to reach the weight at which they make good beef.

A very important factor in the production of good meat is the treatment an animal receives at slaughter time, and how that meat is stored afterwards. Body chemistry means that an animal that is calm and rested when killed produces meat that keeps better, cooks better and tastes better. Keeping is particularly important for beef, lamb, mutton and pork, which are allowed to 'hang' in controlled, cool conditions. This process (also called maturing, aging or conditioning) allows changes in the meat to take place, increasing both the flavour and tenderness. Sheep and pigs are hung for relatively short periods of time, around 1 week. Beef may be hung for anything between 10 days and 4 weeks, although it is rare to find it aged for so long now, as the process occupies valuable space and evaporation means that the meat loses weight, thus increasing the price to the consumer. If you can buy beef aged for 3–4 weeks, it should be very good.

Because of the time and space needed, and the potential for loss of weight during the maturing process, vacuum-packaging is often used by companies both large and small. It is claimed that meat undergoes something akin to the maturing process when vacuum-packed. Meat in vacuum packs is, of course, much easier to handle and store.

Where to buy meat
Who is likely to sell good meat for roasting? To some extent, finding a good supplier needs trial and error. When buying from a supermarket, look for premium lines sourced from specified areas, breeds, groups of farms, or which are given some kind of special treatment (such as proper hanging). Read the labels. The price will almost certainly be a premium one as well. The more anonymous the meat is, the less likely it is to have been raised with care and treated with care. Some of the best meat producers work on a very small scale. To find meat for a good roast, the internet, local producer groups and food and drink festivals are all good sources of information.

One way to source good meat is to get it directly from the farmer who produced it. Direct marketing schemes, farm shops and farmers' markets have educated consumers about some aspects of meat production and have also allowed them to ask, and sometimes to see, how the animals are reared. If you are lucky enough to find such a producer, you will increase your knowledge both of how meat is produced and treated, and may be introduced to suppliers of all sorts of other food.

Alternatively, try to find a butcher you trust. The Q Guild is an organisation of butchers whose members are committed to excellence. Good butchers will be able to provide much more than a slice of rump steak and a couple of chops. They should be able to prepare a joint neatly, deboning it if asked (then giving the bones to you along with the meat, of course); do any trimming and tying as necessary; and be able to provide extra beef or pork fat should the meat require it. They should stock breast of lamb and brisket for inexpensive weekday roasts. And they should also have some knowledge of the food chain that has produced their meat. Most take great pride in the quality of the meat they sell, and specialise in meat from particular animal breeds or areas. Some have a close working relationship with the farmers who raise the meat, or they may even 'finish' sheep and cattle themselves, grazing them until they reach their specifications. Game requires a special licence, which not all butchers hold; fishmongers may hold game licences. A farmers' market may be the best resort. Some specialist game dealers send items by post or courier, and may be best for really unusual items, such as snipe, woodcock or certain species of deer.

Cuts of meat

When you have found a supplier, what should you buy? With a very few exceptions (such as a small rack of lamb), it is a waste of time to roast any piece of meat weighing less than 1kg (2lb 4oz). If the roast is just for two, then there will be leftovers, and there are plenty of dishes to make with those. As a very basic rule of thumb, allow about 125g (4oz) per person for meat off the bone and 250g (9oz) per person for meat on the bone, but don't be too exact about this.

The most sought-after roasts are what are known as 'prime cuts', which have a large proportion of tender lean meat and little, or relatively little, connective tissue. They come mostly from the hindquarters of animals. There is a limited supply and a lot of demand, so they are expensive. Secondary cuts, such as shoulder of pork or shoulder of lamb or mutton, are quite fatty with complex muscle structure and more connective tissue; these still make good roasts, but they don't carve as elegantly. Beef brisket and breast of veal, lamb or mutton are well flavoured; they have a layered structure that can make them chewy, but still make good family meals. Belly pork, which might also be considered, is more tender and seems to be enjoying a revival of interest at present. In general terms, when buying fresh meat that is cut to order, look at the colour of the meat and the texture of the fat, and avoid meat with a lot of juice running from it, or that has an unpleasant smell.

Bones in meat help to conduct heat, so may shorten the cooking times a little. They add flavour, especially to gravy, are useful for making stock and can look impressive when the meat comes to the table. However, they make carving more complex, especially in joints such as shoulder of lamb or mutton. Joints such as rack of lamb and loin of pork should be chined – that is, part of the backbone removed – making them easier to carve. Most joints can be boned and rolled by a butcher on request (if you don't feel equal to the task), leaving a cavity for stuffing. Take the bones home for the stockpot.

Fatty meat has been considered a public enemy by nutritionists for up to 40 years, and eating too much fat is certainly not a good idea. But leanness can be overdone too. A roasting joint needs fat; it is fat that gives much of the flavour to meat, and prevents it becoming dry during cooking. Some will be present in layers on the outside, or between individual muscles; 'marbling' will be visible as streaks and flecks of fat in the lean meat, especially in beef. If fat worries you, remember that some of it will cook out of the meat during roasting and can be skimmed off the juices and then discarded. Visible fat can be cut off your own portion, but don't expect everyone to follow your example.

Meat often arrives vacuum-packed, especially if it has come from a farmers' market or been sent by post. This does produce an odd smell on opening – not actively bad, but one that I would describe as dank and vaguely seaweedy. This can be minimised by opening the pack 1–2 hours before use. Discard any accumulated liquid, pat the meat dry with kitchen paper, put it on a plate and cover loosely with foil or a cloth, then leave it to breathe.

Check the 'use by' date if there is one, and keep meat in the refrigerator or freezer. Vacuum-packed meat can be frozen to extend its keeping time. Meat will keep well for relatively long periods of time in a deep freeze at a temperature of -18°C (0°F). It is important that frozen meat is properly thawed before cooking. Most pieces will thaw overnight at cool room temperature, although if the joint is very large, or the weather very cold, more time may be necessary. The process can be hastened by putting the meat in cold water (not warm) or by using a microwave. Put the meat in a container large enough to catch the 'drip'. Discard this and dry the surface of the meat before cooking.

Poultry and game

Most poultry and game birds arrive wrapped in cling film. Remove the packaging as soon as possible, dry the bird with kitchen paper and pluck out any extraneous feathers. With game birds, the packaging makes it difficult to ascertain how cleanly they have been shot and how old they are – only young birds are suitable for roasting. It also prevents you smelling them to tell how 'high' they are. Find a butcher or game dealer who can be trusted to supply good-quality birds, unless you know a gamekeeper or go shooting and are prepared to dress the birds yourself.

Roasting equipment

A sturdy tin of heavy-gauge metal is essential. Tins come in a range of sizes, from small chop ones to ones that will hold a turkey. Use a tin just large enough to hold the meat comfortably, with a little space around it to allow for basting. If the tin is too large, the cooking juices will dry out and burn. A range of materials is also available: anodized aluminium is a good option if heavy steel is too expensive. A light, thin metal tin will do the job of containing the meat in the oven but may warp when you put it over heat to make gravy. Oval, enamelled, lidded 'self-basting' tins are fairly solid and big enough for most purposes.

For chickens, and for slow-roasting and pot-roasting boned and rolled meat, a deep cast-iron pot with a lid is useful as is a rack that fits inside a large tin, especially for roasting ducks or geese. A two-pronged fork helps when manipulating hot roasts. A carving fork is fine for this.

A supply of kitchen string, both thin and medium-thick, a few metal meat skewers and kitchen foil are necessities. You may also want to invest in a larding needle and a trussing needle, and perhaps a meat thermometer, too, and one of the devices that are available for aiding the removal of fat from gravy. A nice large serving platter or a traditional meat plate look good at the table, but I find a board the best thing to carve on, especially for slicing boned and rolled joints. A good carving knife and fork are essentials. The knife must be sharp, so you will need something to sharpen it with – a patent knife sharpener, a steel or a whetstone.

Preparing a roast

Roasting has a specialist vocabulary all of its own as well as associated techniques, which all add finesse to the results and are well worth learning. Overleaf I explain these techniques and how they will enhance your skills as a cook and the results you achieve.

Barding and larding add extra fat to very lean meat before cooking. Barding is covering the surface of the meat with thin slices of fat, such as bacon draped over a turkey breast. Bacon for barding should be unsmoked, streaked with fat and thinly cut. Pancetta is an option for small, quickly cooked items such as game birds. Beef or pork fat can be cut into thin sheets for encasing lean cuts, or cut into strips and arranged over the meat in a criss-cross pattern. The fat will need to be tied on to the meat with string before cooking. Larding involves inserting lardons, or slivers of fat, into the meat at regular intervals. They melt during cooking and provide fat from the inside. Pork-back fat cut into narrow strips is most common but fat bacon can also be used. A joint can be larded by making incisions with a knife and inserting strips of fat (as sprigs of rosemary and slivers of garlic are inserted into a leg of lamb), but a larding needle gives a better result. Some effort may be needed to draw the needle and fat through the meat. Push the needle away from you, and don't stand near the work surface when you are larding meat. Larding can also be used for adding flavour. Roll the lardons in ground spices or finely chopped herbs, to carry flavour into the meat.

Trussing isn't really necessary with oven roasting. In the past, skewers or string were the norm. Trussing keeps meat, especially poultry and game birds, neat and tidy during cooking, drawing the wings and legs of the bird close to the body. Discard elastic bands before starting to cook.

Marinating A marinade can be as simple as a little olive oil and lemon juice with a couple of thyme sprigs in which the meat is left for 1–2 hours, or an elaborate mixture of wine, herbs and vegetables in which the meat soaks for several days. With a few exceptions, very liquid marinades are probably not a good idea for roasting joints, because they leave the meat soggy, but rubbing the surface with flavourings such as ground spices can be effective. It is sometimes claimed that marinades with acid ingredients help to tenderise meat. The effect is fairly superficial, but they do add flavour, and some marinades help to extend the shelf life of uncooked meat by a couple of days – useful in the past, before refrigeration.

Stuffing Boned joints, poultry and game give you the opportunity to add a layer of stuffing or forcemeat (a forcemeat or farce is more elaborate and fine-textured). It is a technique that was fully exploited in previous centuries. Stuffing can add flavours and fat, provide contrasts in taste and colour, and make a roast go further. Old-fashioned stuffing recipes tend to be quite dense and heavy, but this was deliberate. A texture similar to that of the cooked meat was the aim, so that the two would cut neatly together. Stuffing had the effect of moistening the inside of a joint, the slowly melting internal fat spreading gradually and evenly through meat turning on a spit – an effect mostly lost in oven roasting. Several mixtures are given here, mostly relatively light and principally for flavouring. Bread-based stuffings should use stale bread – if it is fresh, partially dry it in a low oven. For a light-textured stuffing, tear the bread into small pieces rather than using fine crumbs, and bind with a little melted butter and stock or milk. For a traditional, dense texture, add beef suet (about a quarter of the weight of this to the weight of bread) and bind with 1–2 eggs. Calculate the cooking time to include the weight of the stuffing. Alternatively, cook the stuffing separately, baked in a dish, or made into cakes or balls and fried.

Basting means moistening the meat as it cooks, usually by spooning over the juices and fat rendered during cooking, or extra butter, wine or other liquid. The general idea is to help keep the meat moist by returning to it some of the fat that cooks out during roasting and to add flavour. It is less necessary with oven roasting than it was with spit-roasting, but most meat will benefit from occasional basting. Basting is particularly useful for poultry and game birds, as it helps to develop a crisp and delicious finish to the skin.

Dredging and frothing are methods for finishing a joint to give it a crisp surface. Dredging means adding a coating, usually of breadcrumbs (with or without flavourings), during the final stages of cooking. Frothing is dusting plain flour over the meat a few minutes before the end of roasting. If done with a light hand, the veil of flour effectively fries in the fat on the surface of the meat, literally frothing in the process; this also helps give a crisp, tasty finish to the skin. Too much flour won't cook, and gives what Eliza Acton in the 19th century described as 'an objectionable raw taste'. Sometimes flour is rubbed over a joint at the start of roasting to help the fat crisp.

Pot roasting is one step removed from true roasting. It is used for cooking meat in a close-fitting covered container, with flavouring vegetables and aromatics plus a little liquid over gentle heat – braising, in other words. It is useful for meat that tends to be dry and tough otherwise.

Resting Meat cooked at a high temperature, or fast roasted, benefits from 'resting' after cooking. This means leaving it on a warmed serving platter, preferably covered, in a warm place (next to the cooker, or in the grill compartment) for about 20 minutes, or longer with large pieces of meat. It is especially recommended for beef. The texture of the meat evens out, making it better to eat. It also gives you oven space for Yorkshire puddings or to finish browning roast potatoes, and time to fiddle around making gravy, sauces or cooking vegetables at the last minute.

Ovens, temperatures and timings

Getting to know your oven is important for producing a perfect roast. The quirks of individual ovens make it difficult to predict exact cooking times and temperatures. The all-round 'soaking' heat of Agas and similar stoves makes them very good for slow, even, thorough cooking. Electric ovens are generally even in temperature throughout, and manufacturers make claims about the efficiency of fan-assisted ones. Gas ovens can be blazing hot at the top and cooler at the bottom, meaning that items must be moved around on the shelves during cooking. If you lack confidence with a new oven, begin with something good-natured and relatively simple – slow-roast pork or a boned shoulder of lamb – and eat it with new potatoes. There is no point getting hot and bothered over a huge and expensive sirloin of beef, Yorkshire pudding and roast potatoes.

As a rule, beef, lamb, mutton and game may be cooked to any stage between rare and well done, depending on taste, but pork and poultry should always be fully cooked. Joints of meat vary in weight and shape, and people vary in the extent to which they like meat cooked. Prime cuts can be cooked quickly at high temperatures, but lesser ones need longer roasting at lower temperatures. Roasting time for meat is often calculated by allowing a certain amount of time per pound of meat, multiplied by the weight of the joint; this rule of thumb was worked out about 150 years ago when imperial measurements were the norm, and to convert it to metric, remember that 500g is roughly equivalent to 1lb. Times and temperatures given in the sections on individual meats and recipes are guides.

Meat thermometers

One way to make sure a joint is cooked is to use a meat thermometer. Insert it into a thick part of the roast before it goes in the oven (make sure it's not touching any bones) and check the reading as cooking progresses. Probe thermometers are also available – these cannot be put in the oven but can be used to take a reading of the internal temperature of the meat if it is removed from the oven. Avoid any bones when using these and withdraw the probe fairly slowly.

Gravy

'Gravy,' wrote Alan Davidson in The Oxford Companion to Food, 'in the British Isles and areas culturally influenced by them, is … well, gravy, a term fully comprehensible to those who use it, but something of a mystery to the rest of the world.' Possibly some of the confusion is due to changes in the meaning of the word over the last three centuries. It has referred to both concentrated essences derived from cooking large amounts of meat with water and flavourings and the juices that appeared when slashing half-cooked meat on the spit and pressing it; finally, it came to mean a sauce based on the juices left in the roasting tin, or a mixture made with packaged powder and water.

There is a general perception, promoted by the manufacturers of convenience foods, that whatever else gravy is, it should be thick, chestnut brown and plentiful. This isn't always possible by the deglazing method given here, but surely it's better to have a small amount of juice with a really

Most joints produce a certain amount of juice as they cook. Some of this usually browns on the base of the tin, producing delicious flavours – a process known to chemists as the Maillard reaction. These juices can be used to make excellent gravy. The general method is this: remove the meat to a serving platter, then pour any accumulated fat and liquid from the roasting tin into a bowl. The base of the tin will have patches of slightly sticky, well-browned juices on the base and round the edges. These are full of flavour and should not be allowed to go to waste.

Take a little meat stock (or water from cooking vegetables if the former is not available, or even plain water) and pour into the tin. Use a wooden spoon to scrape all the browned patches into the liquid; you may need to put the pan over a low heat. This process is known as deglazing. Once all the residues have been incorporated into the liquid, you can add it to the accumulated cooking juices. Skim off any fat, and use the liquid to make the gravy. Wine, cider or brandy can also be used to deglaze a pan, but they do need to be cooked for a while to mellow the alcohol flavour. Bought stocks can be used although they may not be as good as a well-produced home-made stock.

Carving

Carving is not about simply cutting hunks off a joint of meat. A good carver can make the meat go further, cut it so that it is more tender to eat, and also ensure there are enough leftovers for another dish. Carving divides the meat, helps everyone to similar portions, or to the size of portion they want, retrieves and divides stuffing from the roast, and shares out limited amounts of desirable pieces – the well-roasted outside, the fat that is considered to taste the best, and the most desirable portions of lean meat.

Much of the ceremonial aspect of carving has been lost, which seems a little sad. After all, the meat on the platter probably represents quite an investment for the household in both time and money, as well as a treat for all those who are about to share it, so why not have a bit of ceremony?

Invest in a good set of carvers – that is, a carving knife and fork. The former should have a long, fairly narrow blade with a slightly flexible tip for cutting round bones, and be capable of taking a good edge. The latter will have two long tines, and should have a guard that can be raised to stop the knife blade slipping back up towards your hand. The fork is used for steadying the joint (try not to stab it deeply and make puncture marks); the knife, if properly sharp, will do most of the work.

When carving, always bear in mind the direction of the grain of the meat (the muscle fibres) and, as much as possible, cut across it. Joints without bone, such as beef fillet or topside, are very simple to carve, as are any joints that have been boned and rolled. With these, it is simply a case of slicing through the meat as if you are cutting through a Swiss roll (but in much thinner slices – chunky slices of roast are not especially pleasant to eat).

Accompaniments

Covering a pie

THE METHOD is essentially the same, whether using shortcrust or puff pastry.

Use a traditional English pie or pudding dish with an edge about 1cm (½ in) wide. Put in the filling, and allow it to cool if it is hot. A pie funnel in the centre is a nice traditional touch, especially in large pies. Roll out the pastry on a floured surface to just over 5mm (¼in) thick, aiming for a shape roughly equivalent to the dish, but a little larger. From this, cut a strip about 1.5cm (⅝in) wide, long enough to go around the edge of the dish.

Using a pastry brush dipped in water, wet the edge of the dish all the way round, then stick the pastry strip to it. Trim the rest of the pastry to the size of the top of the dish. Wet the top of the pastry strip, then cover with the rest of the pastry. Press the two layers lightly together with your fingers (shortcrust pastry can be crimped; cut nicks in the edge of puff pastry to scallop the edge). Cut an air vent in the middle or make a hole where the pie funnel is. Gather together any scraps of pastry, re-roll and cut into leaves or other shapes as desired, then wet the reverse and use to decorate the pie.

Brush the top of the pie lightly with beaten egg, or a little cream or milk. Put shortcrust-covered pies into a moderately hot oven at 200°C (400°F, Gas mark 6) for about 20 minutes, then turn the heat down to 180°C (350°F, Gas mark 4) to complete the cooking. Puff pastry needs to rise as well as cook through. Start this in a hot oven at 220°C (425°F, Gas mark 7), turning down to 180°C (350°F, Gas mark 4) for the remainder of cooking time.

The pie dish can be lined with pastry before the filling is added if desired, but gravy makes it soft, and it can be difficult to get the lower crust properly browned in the centre. Using a metal pie dish and putting it on a hot baking sheet before cooking helps.

Puff Pastry

This recipe is a simplified version, known in British cookery as 'rough puff pastry'. It won't rise as much as true puff pastry but is still good. The fat must be cold from the fridge. Use a sharp knife to cut the pastry, and don't crush the cut edges or get egg wash on them, or it won't rise as nicely.

250g (9oz) flour, plus extra for dusting and rolling

175g (6oz) chilled fat (equal quantities of butter and lard

iced water

½ tsp salt

Put the flour and salt in a bowl. Coarsely grate the butter and lard into the flour, then start adding iced water, a tablespoon at a time, stirring with your hand to a stiff paste. Don't overdo the water: the mixture should not be sticky.

On a floured surface, work the mixture until it's even. Roll into an oblong three times as long as it is wide; turn the top third down towards you and the bottom third up to cover this. Turn 90 degrees clockwise and repeat the rolling and folding. Chill for 30 minutes. Repeat the rolling and folding twice more, then give the pastry a final rest. If made a day in advance, wrap in foil or clingfilm and chill overnight.

Shortcrust Pastry

Use lard for a very short pastry or butter for good flavour – or a mixture of both.

300g (11oz) flour mixed with a generous pinch of salt

150g (5oz) lard, butter, or lard and butter mixed

6–8 tablespoons cold water

Put the flour and salt in a bowl. Cut the fat into 1cm (½in) dice and lightly rub into the flour with your fingertips until the mixture resembles fine breadcrumbs. Add enough water to make a coherent dough. Shape it into a ball, wrap in foil and put in a cool place for at least 30 minutes to rest before using.

Dumplings

Suet dumplings are comforting companions for a meaty stew, particularly one made with beef. They probably share a common ancestor with suet puddings, and are rib-sticking food intended to stretch precious supplies of other, more expensive ingredients. They are simple to make and easy to vary with different flavourings. Make the mixture just before you want to cook it. Plain flour mixed with 1 teaspoon baking powder can be used instead of self-raising flour if desired. The stew they are destined for needs to be completely cooked. Bear in mind that the dumplings will need about 25 minutes to cook after they have been added.

serves
4

120g (4oz) self-raising flour
60g (2¼oz) shredded suet
about 120ml (4fl oz) water, to mix
a pinch of salt

To flavour
1 generous tablespoon chopped parsley
with a little thyme and marjoram;

or 1 generous teaspoon mustard powder and about 1 tablespoon chopped parsley or chives; or 1 generous tablespoon creamed horseradish; or a little chopped fresh tarragon

If you are reheating a stew, it is best to start this off before adding the dumplings. Put all the dry ingredients into a bowl. Add the flavouring ingredients if desired. Then add about two-thirds of the water and mix. The mixture should be fairly soft but not too sticky. Add a little more water if it seems dry. Form into balls the size of a large walnut and drop them on top of the stew.

If the stew is cooking in the oven, leave it uncovered after adding the dumplings. They will crisp slightly on top, and may colour a little in the heat. If the stew is cooking on the hob, drop the dumplings into the liquid and cover the pan.

Cook for a further 20–30 minutes in the oven on 180°C, 350°F, Gas mark 4 until the dumplings are cooked through and slightly golden on top. Alternatively, allow about 20 minutes for a stew cooking on the hob.

TIP: For dumplings to be cooked on top of a stew in the oven, try replacing 40g (1½oz) of the flour with 40g (1½oz) dried breadcrumbs – this makes the surface crisper.

Norfolk Dumplings

Norfolk dumplings are made from ordinary bread dough. Instead of baking in the conventional manner, the dough is cooked in boiling water. They make a good accompaniment to stews with a generous amount of strongly flavoured gravy, such as those based on game.

serves
6

1 teaspoon dried yeast
150ml (5fl oz) hand-hot water
250g (9oz) flour, plus extra for dusting
1 scant teaspoon salt

Add the yeast to the water and leave in a warm place for a few minutes until frothy. Stir the yeast mixture into the flour and salt and knead well, then allow it to rise for about 1 hour or until doubled in size.

Have ready a large pot of boiling salted water. Divide the dough into six, make into balls and drop into the water. Keep them boiling for about 20–25 minutes. The dumplings will expand a little as they cook. Drain and serve with the stew. Don't try to cut them, but pull apart with two forks.

Cobbler Topping for Stew

This is a soft dough cut into rounds and placed in a layer over a stew or other sauce. The idea found its way into English recipe books in the 1960s and 1970s as an alternative to dumplings or pastry. The dough is reminiscent of a savoury scone mix – or perhaps one should say a North American biscuit dough, since the idea seems to have come from there. You can use it instead of dumplings with beef and vegetable stews or instead of pastry on game pies. As with dumplings, the stew should be almost cooked or heated through before the topping is added, and cooking needs to be finished off in the oven.

serves
4

150g (5oz) plain flour, plus extra for
    rolling out
2 teaspoons baking powder
pinch salt
30g (1oz) butter
1 egg, beaten
1–2 tablespoons milk

Sift the flour, baking powder and salt together. Rub in the butter. Mix to a soft dough with the egg, adding a little milk if necessary.

Roll out to 2cm (¾in) thick and cut into rounds 5cm (2in) in diameter. Arrange these over the top of the stew – some people try to overlap them so that the edges crisp a little, browning and adding contrasts of texture. Brush the tops with milk.

Turn the oven up to 230°C, 450°F, Gas mark 8 and cook for 15–20 minutes, or until the topping is well risen and brown. Keep an eye on it to make sure it doesn't burn.

Forcemeat Balls and Butterballs

Forcemeat balls are considerably more elegant than dumplings. They are a traditional garnish for many game dishes and were also added to pie fillings. In the past they were usually fried, but can be cooked in the oven if preferred. Forcemeat balls can also be made very small. It took me years to realise that 'butterballs' – small delicate dumplings my mother served in soups – were essentially forcemeat balls made without flavourings.

serves
4

120g (4oz) fresh breadcrumbs
60g (2¼oz) butter
1 egg yolk
zest of 2 large lemons
3 tablespoons chopped parsley
1 tablespoon chopped thyme leaves
a generous grating of nutmeg
1 teaspoon salt
black pepper
butter, for frying

To make the forcemeat, put all the ingredients into the goblet of a food processor or blender. Process for a few seconds to give a smooth paste. Shape this into walnut-sized balls and fry them gently in butter, turning frequently, for about 10 minutes. Add them to the stew before serving.

Alternatively, put them into a baking dish and bake in the oven for about 20 minutes on 180°C, 350°F, Gas mark 4.

For butterballs, use only the breadcrumbs, butter, egg yolk and a pinch of salt. Make them very small – the size of hazelnuts – and poach gently in a stew for the last 5–10 minutes. They are excellent with fish or vegetable stews.

Mashed Potatoes

I can't remember where I first came across this version, but I think it was in a 19th-century book and the writer stated that it was the way the French made mashed potato.

serves
4

500g (1lb 2oz) potatoes
30g (1oz) unsalted butter
salt and pepper

Peel the potatoes, then cut into chunks and boil as usual. When tender, do not pour the cooking water down the sink, but drain it into a jug.

Add the butter to the potatoes and season with salt and pepper. Mash the potatoes, adding a little of the reserved cooking water and continuing to mash, adding more cooking water if necessary, or butter if you want, until you feel they have achieved the right consistency.

Potatoes Roast in Cream and Herbs

This is not a traditional method for roasting potatoes, but it is very good with just about any meat, especially game dishes.

serves
4–6

2–3 fresh rosemary sprigs about
   6cm (2½in) long
8–10 fresh sage leaves
12 fresh thyme sprigs
1–2 garlic cloves, peeled

750g (1lb 10oz) potatoes, peeled
   and cut in 2cm (¾in) chunks
200ml (7fl oz) double cream
1 teaspoon salt
freshly ground black pepper

Preheat the oven to 200°C, 400°F, Gas mark 6.

Strip the leaves off the rosemary and chop them together with the sage, thyme and garlic. Mix the potatoes, cream, chopped herb mixture, salt and some pepper. Put them in an ovenproof dish or small roasting tin that holds them comfortably in a shallow layer.

Cook for about 30 minutes, stirring once or twice. By the end of this time, they should be tender (give them a little longer if not), and the cream should be thick, clinging to the potatoes, and lightly flecked with gold on the surface.

Roast Parsnips

This is a root that goes well with roast beef. Parsnips are considered to be at their best in winter, after the first frosts – freezing temperatures convert some of the starch in the living roots into sugar, and this caramelises when they are cooked.

serves 4–6

about 50g (2oz) fat for roasting,
   such as dripping from beef
   or pork or lard

about 500g (1–1½lb) parsnips,
   washed, trimmed and peeled
salt

Cut the parsnips diagonally into slices 5mm (¼in) thick. Parboil for 5 minutes if wished. Put the fat in a roasting tin in a hot oven at 220°C, 425°F, Gas mark 7.

Drain the parsnips well if parboiled, then tip into the hot fat. Turn them in the fat, sprinkle with a little salt, and roast for 10 minutes. Turn the heat down to 190°C, 375°F, Gas mark 5, and cook for 20–30 minutes, stirring occasionally so they develop nicely browned surfaces. Drain well before serving.

Game Chips

These need maincrop potatoes, preferably ones that are long and quite regular in shape; Maris Piper are a variety that works reasonably well.

serves 2–3

Peel some potatoes and trim off any irregular edges. Cut into very narrow strips, 2mm (¹⁄₁₆in) thick and the same wide, and as long as the potatoes allow. Drop them into a bowl of cold water and leave to soak for 15 minutes. Drain and spread on a cloth or kitchen paper and dry them thoroughly.

Heat the oil in a deep-fat fryer to 180–185°C (350–360°F). Alternatively, drop a small cube of bread into the hot fat and if it rises to the surface and browns in 30 seconds, the fat is hot enough (don't let it get to smoking point, which is too hot). Fry the chips in batches until golden, then remove with a slotted spoon and drain well on kitchen paper. Sprinkle with sea salt flakes and serve.

Sage and Onion Stuffing

This recipe – suitable for pork, goose or duck – was considered old-fashioned by the 1840s. It was also thought too overpowering by Victorian cooks, although Eliza Acton remarked that some people always liked it with a leg of pork (which was stuffed at the knuckle end). It has outlived the Victorians and remains one of the most iconic mixtures in the English kitchen. In her otherwise excellent recipe on which the one below is based, Mrs Roundell in *Mrs Roundell's Practical Cookery Book* (1898), suggested that a very few well-blanched sage leaves were sufficient. We are accustomed to much bigger flavours, so I have added a few more and omitted the blanching. A mixture based on one onion is about the right amount for stuffing a duck but you should double it for a goose.

serves 4–6

1 large onion, peeled
12 fresh sage leaves, washed
60g (2½oz) stale breadcrumbs
20g (¾oz) unsalted butter, cut in
    small pieces (or beef suet for a
    traditional mixture)

1 medium egg, beaten
½ teaspoon salt
a little freshly ground black pepper

Put the onion in a pan, cover with boiling water and simmer for 20–30 minutes, or until tender. Drain. Once it is cool enough to handle, cut it into quarters. Put it in a food processor with the sage and chop (but don't reduce it to a purée), or chop together by hand until fairly fine. Stir in the breadcrumbs, butter and enough egg to bind lightly, then stir in the seasoning (don't use the processor, which makes the mixture too runny).

Use to stuff a boned and rolled pork roast or a bird, or press into a greased dish and bake along with the roast for the last 30 minutes of cooking time.

Chestnut and Prune Stuffing

Chestnut stuffing is more commonly associated with turkey, but it can also be very good with goose. The same is true for prunes, which are quite often used with goose in continental Europe. Like potato stuffing, this combination didn't make much of an impact in British cookery until the mid-20th century.

serves 6–8

15g (½oz) unsalted butter
1–2 shallots, peeled and finely chopped
1 garlic clove, peeled and crushed
200–250g (7–9oz) chestnut purée
   (tinned is fine)
200–250g (7–9oz) sausage meat
about 12 prunes (ready-to-eat, or
   soaked dried ones), pitted

2 large apples (Cox's or a dryish,
   aromatic eating apple), peeled,
   cored and cut in thick slices
1 scant teaspoon salt
freshly ground black pepper

Melt the butter in a small pan and fry the shallots and garlic lightly. Put the chestnut purée in a bowl and break it up. Mix in the shallots and garlic, sausage meat, salt and a generous seasoning of pepper.

Put half this mixture into the goose, then add the prunes and apples in a layer, and spread the remainder of the stuffing over them.

Dried Apricot and Almond Stuffing

While lamb or mutton cooked on the bone scores best for flavour, it is not the easiest thing to carve. Both leg and shoulder are often boned, creating joints ideal for stuffing. This recipe uses a fruit and nut combination derived from Arab cookery. Stuff the joint, then roll and tie with string. Or, if using a boned shoulder, tie it as a 'cushion' – in four, like a parcel – or as a 'melon'; manoeuvre the stuffed meat into a rough ball shape, then take a long piece of string and wrap it four times round the meat, crossing at the poles, giving the appearance of eight sections like a cantaloupe melon. Carve a rolled joint into slices, and a cushion or melon into sections.

serves 3–4

40g (1½oz) unsalted butter
1 small onion, peeled and very finely chopped
50g (2oz) almonds, blanched and cut into slivers
150g (5oz) crustless day-old white bread, torn into small pieces
75g (3oz) dried apricots, soaked for a few hours, then drained and chopped roughly

zest of ½ lemon (preferably unwaxed), finely grated
a generous pinch of freshly grated nutmeg
50–100ml (2–3½fl oz) stock or milk
½ teaspoon salt
freshly ground black pepper

Melt the butter in a small frying pan and sauté the onion gently until translucent. Toast the almonds lightly in the oven for 5–10 minutes; watch to make sure they don't burn. In a bowl, combine the onion, almonds, bread, apricots and lemon zest. Season with a generous grating of nutmeg, the salt and some pepper. Mix well and pour in just enough stock or milk to make the bread moist but not soggy.

Use to stuff the cavity left by boning the joint and then roast as directed in the recipe. Alternatively, make the stuffing mixture into small balls and bake in a lightly greased dish for about 20–30 minutes at 180°C, 350°F, Gas mark 4.

Mint Sauce

By the mid-20th century, mint sauce seemed to be the preferred accompaniment for lamb, combining two elements that go well with this meat – a strongly aromatic perfume and a sharp taste. Unfortunately, it was often badly made. For mint sauce lovers, Eliza Acton's recipe of 3 heaped teaspoons of finely chopped young fresh mint, 2 heaped teaspoons of caster sugar and 6 teaspoons of 'the best vinegar' (try a good white wine one) is a good formula. Stir together until the sugar has dissolved.

Orange Sauce for Roast Duck

Over the centuries, many cultures have devised ways for cooking and serving duck with fruity and sweet–acid flavours. Seville (bitter, or marmalade) oranges are best, with both tame and wild duck. Their season is very limited – they come on to the market in mid-December and vanish by the end of January – but they can be frozen. This orange sauce is based on one given by Martha Bradley in 1756.

100ml (3½fl oz) port
the cooking juices from the bird,
   skimmed of fat

juice of 2 Seville oranges
juice of 1 lemon
salt and pepper

Deglaze the roasting tin with the port and pour all into a small pan. Add the juices from cooking the bird and the orange and lemon juice, and bring to the boil. Taste, and season with salt and pepper. Serve with the duck and a sweetish vegetable accompaniment, such as roast parsnips, or perhaps boiled potatoes and boiled parsnips mashed together.

A Sauce for Cold Meat

The original of this was given as 'A sauce for Partridge, or Moor Game' in the pompously named *Culina Famulatrix Medicinæ* published by Ignotus (otherwise known as Dr A. Hunter) in 1807. It produces a surprisingly modern result, and is also delicious with roast meat.

4 salted anchovies, well rinsed
2 fat garlic cloves, peeled
juice of ½ lemon (you may not
   need all this)

180ml (6fl oz) olive oil
cold roast meat, cut in small,
   neat pieces
freshly ground black pepper

Put the anchovies, garlic, half the lemon juice and the oil in a blender and whizz together. Taste, and add more lemon juice if you wish; you might also like to add some pepper, although it is unlikely that any salt will be needed.

Mix with the roast meat. Serve this on a bed of salad leaves or with lightly cooked French beans, or broccoli spears, or small new potatoes.

Apple Sauce

Apple sauce is a traditional accompaniment for pork and goose. It is very simple to make: peel and core 2 large Bramley apples, then cut into small pieces. Cook gently in a small pan with just enough water to prevent them from sticking. Stir frequently. Once they have become a purée, add about 3 teaspoons of sugar, or enough to taste.

Caramelised Apples

These are good served with pork, goose or duck. If serving with duck, add a little grated orange zest at the end. The apples must be a firm-fleshed type that will keep their shape when cooked.

serves
4–6

30g (1oz) unsalted butter
3 large apples (Cox's or a dryish,
    aromatic eating apple), peeled,
    cored and sliced, but not too thinly

a piece of star anise (optional)
1 dessertspoon cider vinegar
2 tablespoons sugar

Melt the butter in a heavy frying pan and add the apple slices, and the star anise if using. Cook gently, stirring frequently, until the apple is softening and has become slightly transparent. Add the cider vinegar, then the sugar and continue to cook until the apple begins to caramelise. Serve tepid.

Cumberland Sauce

A delicious sauce for cold ham or game. It appears to have no links with the county of that name, and a legend associating it with the royal title of the Duke of Cumberland appears to be just that – a legend. The base of redcurrant jelly and wine is reminiscent of 18th-century sauces for venison, but the first recognisable recipe was given (under a different name) by Alexis Soyer in 1853. It seems to have been the French chef Georges Auguste Escoffier who popularised the recipe and made it a commercial success in the 19th century.

serves 4–6

zest of 1 orange (preferably unwaxed), cut in thin strips

zest of 1 lemon (preferably unwaxed), cut in thin strips

4 tablespoons redcurrant jelly

4 tablespoons port

1 teaspoon smooth Dijon mustard

a pinch of ground ginger

Put the orange and lemon zest in a small bowl, then cover with boiling water and leave to blanch for 3–4 minutes. Drain well.

Melt the jelly in a small pan, stirring to smooth out any lumps. Add the port and mix well. Stir in the zest, the mustard and a little ginger. Taste and add a little more mustard or ginger if desired. Allow to cool before serving with cold meat.

Beef and Veal

BEEF HAS LONG STOOD FOR ALL THINGS GOOD about food in England, excellent in quality and abundant in supply. To celebrate extraordinary events, whole oxen were roasted as on the ice of the Thames during the Frost Fairs of the 17th and 18th centuries. On a domestic scale, a roast sirloin or rump of beef was considered the best of food. Privileged aristocrats and their French cooks had game and fancy dishes – but plain food was the natural food of the true upstanding Englishman. The motif of roast beef appears again and again, in cartoons, prints, in the kitchen scenes depicted in recipe books, in menus real and imagined. Roast beef and Yorkshire pudding is still an ideal Sunday dinner. The pudding might once have been a plum pudding and now it's always Yorkshire – but the beef remains the same.

Attitudes towards veal were more ambivalent than those towards beef. Veal used to be a sought after ingredient, especially in French influenced *haute cuisine*, but over the years, and especially in the 20th century, welfare concerns were raised about the conditions in which veal calves were reared, demand fell and it is not so widely available now, although it's coming back into vogue.

Homely stews of well-cooked beef with a few onions and gravy date back to the 17th century. Over the centuries, the liquid used has varied from wine, beer, vinegar or stock to just water, and the seasoning from onions, garlic or spices to the popular proprietary sauces of the 19th century. The idea remains the same though the method has changed; originally, the meat was gently cooked, placed between two dishes and set over the embers. Steaks in the past were normally cut from a rump of beef, an alternative to stewing it as a large piece of meat. Large joints were boiled with herbs and root vegetables in the 17th century. For the elegant dishes introduced in the 18th century, the meat received all the standard treatments of cooks in great houses. The names of the dishes (*à la braise, à la daube, à la mode, à la royale*) give away their French origin. They were rich and savoury with wine, spices, herbs, bacon or ham, beef gravy (stock), garnishes of morels and truffles and luxurious morsels. Except for Beef à la Mode, they were largely forgotten by the 19th century, although their descendants, such as *Boeuf à la Bourguignonne*, were periodically rediscovered in France by English cooks. The modest beef stews of the type we know, with onions and root vegetables, emerged by the 19th century.

Beef steaks were also regarded as good fillings for pies, earlier ones being elaborate and often involving highly seasoned forcemeat. This element disappeared in the 18th century, although oysters were frequently added until disease and pollution eradicated most of the fisheries in the mid-19th century. Steak and kidney pie, now an iconic English dish, was developing in this period, as were pastry-covered meat and potato pies and the mashed potato-topped cottage pie.

Attitudes to veal have become complicated in recent years, but there are numerous recipes in old books. Valued for its pale colour and delicate flavour, it was made into fricassées, cooked with spring vegetables, or served braised or with a ragoo. The English tradition also includes many recipes for olives of veal, rolled around stuffing mixtures and cooked alone or made into veal and ham pies.

Both beef and veal were essential as the foundations for many elaborate stews and braises in the 18th century. Beef bones and coarse 'gravy beef' gave both flavour and colour to broths and stocks that were common to all meat dishes. Veal made pale gelatinous stocks that could be slowly reduced to glazes, covering the finished dish with a transparent glistening coat.

Cooking beef in stews and pies

Beef for stewing or braising is generally cut from the forequarter of the animal. This provides stewing and braising steak from the neck and shoulder, and shin, which has a characteristic patterning of collagen through the slices. Shin is good for very slow-cooked stews, in which the collagen dissolves and adds body to the sauce. The hindquarter also provides meat suitable for braised dishes, particularly from the top rump – this is relatively tender, good in stewed-steak dishes. Flank, although fatty, is also good for slow cooking. Other cuts of beef for stews are skirt, oxtail and ox cheek, all of which require liquid and a low oven for several hours to make them really tender, but they are inexpensive and well-flavoured. Large pieces of beef can be braised. Brisket may have a complex interleaved structure and a tendency to shrink in cooking, but has good flavour. Topside is a more elegant alternative.

Stewing steak can be bought ready diced, although some people prefer to buy a large piece and then trim off the excess fat and cut it into cubes themselves. It doesn't always have to be cut into small pieces; you may prefer to use larger ones, and some stews, such as *Boeuf à la Bourguignonne*, call for it to be cut slightly differently.

A standard English-style stew of beef will take 2–3 hours to cook slowly. For a pie filling, you should cook the meat in its sauce and allow it to cool a little before covering with pastry. Beef shares some characteristics with venison in so far as both are red meats with pronounced flavours that react well to wine and herb sauces and which benefit from slow cooking at lower temperatures. Recipes can be used more or less interchangeably.

Cooking veal in stews and pies

Veal is quite different from beef – pale, delicate, lean and with a tendency to dryness. It is expensive and sometimes difficult to buy, although many good butchers and some supermarkets now stock it, but it can be delicious. Stewing veal can sometimes be purchased ready-diced, or you can buy breast or neck of veal and then trim and cut it up yourself at home. It is also good in fricassée-style sauces.

Try not to overcook the meat – traditional methods of overcoming dryness included larding, cooking the veal with slices of bacon, and adding rich forcemeats. In English traditional cookery, mildly acidic flavours were often used with veal; sorrel was favoured, but you can use lemon juice instead or even gooseberries. For richer, meatier dishes, dry sherry can be a good addition to the cooking liquid.

Buying beef and veal cuts for roasting

Roasting beef is as much about cooking good meat by the correct method for the cut, as about the recipes. Excellent beef is best bought from a good butcher, and the best of all comes from dedicated beef herds grazing on open pasture and will have been allowed to hang for at least three weeks. The lean should be a good, deep red colour (not bright red) and lightly marbled – flecked with streaks of fat. The visible fat should be creamy-white and crumbly in texture.

Veal is a by-product of the dairy industry; anyone who drinks milk or eats cheese, butter, yoghurt or ice cream should not object to eating this meat. Although milk-fed veal at 2½–3 months old is still considered the best, there is an alternative: this is 'rosy', or rosé, veal, a deep pink colour with a light streaking of fat in between the muscles. It comes from older, loose-housed or outdoor-reared calves. Tracking it down takes persistence, and once you find it, you may have to order roasting joints. A butcher who deals with the catering trade, or the internet, are the most likely sources.

What to buy and how much

The British method of butchering beef and veal tends to run across major muscle groups, cutting through the fat and bone (rather than dissecting muscles out, which tends to be the usual practice in continental Europe). In the past, the names for cuts varied quite a lot regionally, although they appear to be fairly standard now.

Sirloin is expensive, and if you want a piece from the rear end of the joint with the fillet still in place, you may have to order it: the joint is more profitable when divided into sirloin, fillet and T-bone steaks. Working forwards, the front part of the sirloin is also known as the wing rib, with a good eye of lean meat but no undercut. Attached to this is the forerib, with streaks and layers of fat in the 'tail', getting progressively less lean. These joints respond well to fast roasting at relatively high temperatures.

Buy sirloin by weight, and rib joints by the number of ribs, although they can be boned and rolled (which makes them easier to carve, but less splendid at the table). A fillet of beef, or a piece of one, will be very expensive and is usually used for Beef Wellington. Brisket (boned and rolled) has an excellent flavour, but it is highly variable in both its size and fat content, and has a tendency towards toughness. It's best to be guided by the butcher's opinion, and treat it gently, with long, slow cooking.

Working back from the sirloin, the next cut is the rump, which is now principally used for steaks; behind this, at the top of the hind leg, lies the topside, a very lean piece of meat that makes a good slow roast; and next to it the silverside and a muscle known as the pope's eye – both of these are also possible roasting joints. These need to be slow roasted or pot roasted.

Veal cuts for roasting include the loin (the equivalent of the sirloin in beef cattle) and, the chump end or fillet and topside; towards the head, the best end (equivalent to a beef rib roast) and the shoulder; the breast can also be boned and rolled with stuffing. When roasting veal, always remember that is very lean and it tends to dry out easily, so you must treat it gently and be sure to use a slow-roast method with secondary cuts.

Storage and preparation

The British have traditionally considered that any home-produced roasting beef is full of flavour and too good to be 'messed around with' – i.e., marinated or otherwise flavoured before cooking – and when cooked appropriately, the meat will be sufficiently tender. As far as flavourings are concerned, beef fillet (less pronounced in flavour than many cuts) can benefit from marinating with oil and herbs, and light spicing makes an interesting change with slow-roast cuts. Otherwise, restrict seasonings to salt and pepper, and possibly a little mustard powder mixed with plain flour and rubbed into the fat of a sirloin or rib roast before cooking. Very lean beef benefits from barding with extra fat.

Veal has a delicate flavour that is easily overpowered by strong seasonings. Good contrasts are light, lemony notes; salted meat such as ham or bacon; the nutty flavours of some fortified wines; and a mild mustard of the Dijon type. Stuffings are a good idea with veal. Because it is from young animals without much fat, veal can be dry. To help prevent this, bard with pork fat or spread a little butter over it before cooking. If you can obtain some veal bones (even in relatively small quantities) and use them to make stock, these will enhance veal gravy and many other dishes.

Times and temperatures

How 'done' should roast beef be? Some people hate well-done beef, whereas others don't like to see any pink in the middle at all. In the mid-20th century, well-done meat seems to have been the norm, but since the 1980s, chefs and cookery writers have shown a very definite preference for underdone meat generally. If you are intending to use some of the roast beef cold or for leftovers, it's better if it is kept slightly rare. Very lean cuts of beef, such as topside, are better if they are done on the rare side of medium, because they tend to dry out during prolonged cooking. Really, it's a matter of taste and you must decide. There are two methods for roasting beef. The first is sometimes known as high-heat or fast roasting. For a fast roast, give the meat 20 minutes at 240°C, 475°F, Gas mark 9, then reduce the heat to 180°C, 350°F, Gas mark 4 and cook for the following times:
- Beef on the bone: 15 minutes per 500g (rare); 18–20 minutes per 500g (medium); 25 minutes per 500g (well done).
- Boneless beef: 12 minutes per 500g (rare); 13–15 minutes per 500g (medium); 20 minutes per 500g (well done).

The second method is slow roasting. Cook at 150°C, 300°F, Gas mark 2 for the entire time, allowing 20–25 minutes per 500g for rare to medium, and 30–35 minutes per 500g for well-done meat. Cook pot roasts even more slowly, at 140°C, 275°F, Gas mark 1, and up to 60 minutes per 500g.

Veal, because it tends to dryness, needs gentle heat. It should always be well done, but be careful not to overcook it. Start it at 190°C, 375°F, Gas mark 5 for 15 minutes, and then turn the heat down to 180°C, 350°F, Gas mark 4 and allow 25–30 minutes per 500g.

Roast Beef and Yorkshire Pudding

serves 6

a piece of sirloin or rib roast,
   or wing rib or forerib
salt and pepper
about 1 tablespoon plain flour
1 teaspoon mustard powder
about 300ml (10fl oz) beef stock

For the pudding
2 eggs, beaten
100g (4oz) plain flour, sifted
a pinch of salt
150ml (5fl oz) milk mixed with
   150ml (5fl oz) water
beef dripping from the roast

Take the beef out of the refrigerator about 1 hour before you want to start cooking it. Preheat the oven to 240°C, 475°F, Gas mark 9. Season a little flour with the mustard powder, salt and pepper and rub it into the fat. Put the meat, bones downward, into a suitable roasting tin and roast for 15 minutes, then reduce the heat to 180°C, 350°F, Gas mark 4. Cook for 15 minutes per 500g (rare); 18–20 minutes per 500g (medium); or 25 minutes per 500g (well done).

While the meat is roasting, prepare the pudding batter. Mix the eggs, flour and salt. Then use a whisk to blend in the milk and water, to make a batter with the consistency of thin cream. Leave to stand.

After the beef has been removed from the oven to rest, turn up the heat to 220°C, 425°F, Gas mark 7. Add 1 generous tablespoon of dripping to the Yorkshire pudding tin and heat it in the oven until smoking hot. Pour in all but about 2 tablespoons of the batter (it should hiss spectacularly if the fat is at the right temperature), and then return the pudding to the oven. Cook for about 30 minutes, until it is well browned in patches and light and crisp in texture.

To make the gravy, take the tin the beef was roasted in and spoon off any excess fat. Deglaze, preferably with stock. Let this bubble, and then, off the heat, stir in the remainder of the Yorkshire pudding batter, and keep stirring until the mixture thickens (you may need to heat it gently to achieve this). Add a little more stock if necessary, then taste and adjust the seasoning.

To follow tradition cut the pudding into squares and eat with gravy before the meat.

Slow Roast Topside

Slow roasting is a good method for lean joints, such as topside, whose low-fat content means they have a tendency to be dry.

serves
6

beef topside, 1.5–2kg (3½lb–4½lb)
extra beef fat, cut in thin slices
    for barding (optional)

about 150ml (5fl oz) beef stock
about 1 tablespoon plain flour
salt and pepper

If you wish to bard the topside, arrange the fat in a layer over the meat and tie it on with string. Put the meat in a roasting tin that it fits reasonably well. Put in a low oven, 150°C, 300°F, Gas mark 2 (use the highest shelf in a gas oven) and allow 25 minutes per 500g for rare to medium-rare meat, 30–35 minutes for well done. About two-thirds of the way through cooking, season the meat with salt.

When the meat is cooked to your taste, remove it from the tin to a hot dish. Snip the strings holding the fat in place and discard them and the remains of the fat (the fat should have cooked through, so you may find it crisp and delicious). Keep the meat warm. Pour the cooking juices out of the roasting tin into a bowl, then deglaze the tin with a little stock and add this to the juices. Skim them, returning 2–3 tablespoons of fat to the roasting tin; stir in a little flour and allow it to cook and brown gently. Stir in the juices, plus stock as necessary, to make the gravy; taste and correct the seasoning, then serve.

Pot-Roast Brisket of Beef

serves
6

2kg (4½lb) piece of rolled brisket
1 tablespoon olive oil
a handful of shallots, peeled
1 garlic clove, peeled and sliced
1 scant tablespoon plain flour
200ml (7fl oz) red wine
about 150ml (5fl oz) beef
   stock (optional)
1 teaspoon salt

For the marinade
2 teaspoons black peppercorns
2 blades of mace
6 cloves
fresh root ginger, about 1cm (½in)
   cube, peeled and finely grated
1 generous dessertspoon
   demerara sugar
1 garlic clove, peeled and crushed

To prepare the marinade, put the peppercorns, mace and cloves in a mortar and crush roughly. Stir in the ginger, sugar and garlic, then rub the beef with this mixture. Cover and leave overnight in a cool place or in the refrigerator.

To cook the meat, wipe the beef to remove most of the ground spices. Heat the oil in a casserole and cook the shallots and garlic briskly, stirring frequently, until they begin to brown slightly. Remove to a dish, then put the beef in the casserole and brown it all over. Then put the shallots and garlic around the meat, sprinkle over the flour and add the wine. It should cover the base of the casserole to a depth of about 2cm (¾in).

Fit a doubled sheet of greaseproof paper neatly across the top of the casserole, trimming it so that it doesn't stick out and burn, then put the lid on over this. Cook very gently for 4 hours; this can be done on the lowest possible heat on top of the stove, or in a low oven at 140°C, 275°F, Gas mark 1. Check occasionally, especially if cooking on top of the stove, and add a little stock if necessary, as the gravy tends to reduce and catch; also, sprinkle the salt over the meat.

When cooked, remove the meat to a serving dish. Pour off the gravy and set it aside for a few minutes, then skim off the fat. You should be left with a glossy, deep-brown, rich-tasting sauce, which can be thinned with a little stock or water if you like. Check the seasoning. Slice the meat thinly, and pass round the gravy and some mashed potatoes.

Beef Stew with Root Vegetables & Dumplings

This stew has been a mainstay of English domestic cookery since the mid-19th century. Make it with whatever cut of beef you prefer, cook it with stock or beer and add root vegetables and dumplings. Comfort food for the coldest winter day.

serves
4

50g (2oz) beef dripping, lard or oil,
    plus a little extra
1 large onion, sliced
2 garlic cloves, peeled and crushed
150g (5oz) turnip, peeled and diced
1 large parsnip, trimmed, peeled
    and cubed
1 large carrot, trimmed, peeled
    and cubed
40g (1½oz) flour
450–500g (1lb–1lb 2oz) stewing beef,
    cut into cubes

250ml (9fl oz) beef stock
250ml (9fl oz) mild beer (optional; use
    beef stock or wine instead if desired)
1 bay leaf
a few sprigs marjoram, or 1 teaspoon
    dried marjoram or oregano
salt and black pepper

For the dumplings
1 quantity suet dumpling mix
    (see page 26) flavoured with
    horseradish, or mustard and parsley

Heat the dripping in a frying pan or casserole. Fry the onion until translucent, then add the garlic and let it cook a little longer. Remove the mixture from the fat and keep on one side. Fry the root vegetables for a few minutes and then add them to the onions.

Mix 1 teaspoon salt with some pepper and flour and toss the beef into it. Brown the meat in the remaining fat (in batches if necessary – don't overcrowd the pan). Add the meat to the vegetables in the casserole.

Sprinkle the remaining seasoned flour into the frying pan to make a roux (add a little extra fat first if necessary). Add the beef stock, stirring well and scraping any bits of sediment off the base of the pan. Stir in the beer, if using, and bring to the boil. Pour over the meat and vegetables, add the bay leaf and marjoram, then cover. Cook in a gentle oven, 150°C, 300°F, Gas mark 2, for about 2 hours.

Make up the dumpling mix.

Remove the casserole from the oven and skim off any excess fat. Taste for seasoning and add more if necessary. Distribute the dumplings over the top. Turn the heat up to 180°C, 350°F, Gas mark 4, and return the dish, uncovered to the oven for about 20 minutes, or until the dumplings are cooked through and starting to crisp slightly on top.

Adapt the recipe as desired. If using cuts such as shin of beef or oxtail, reduce the oven temperature to 140°C, 275°F, Gas mark 1 and cook for about 4 hours.

Beef à la Mode

This appeared in cookery books in the first half of the 18th century, along with other obviously French-derived dishes. It can be served hot or cold. You may want to include a pig's foot, which will help the juices set to a jelly when cool, so they can be chopped and served along with the meat. I have suggested using brisket – not the most elegant cut but it is excellently flavoured.

**serves
8**

about 1.5kg (3lb 4oz) brisket, boned
   and rolled
4–6 anchovy fillets
4 cloves
a blade of mace
6–8 peppercorns
120g (4oz) bacon, cut into matchsticks
150ml (5fl oz) red wine
300ml (10fl oz) strong beef stock

4–6 small shallots
1 garlic clove, peeled but left whole
a bouquet garni made from a bay leaf,
   rosemary, thyme and basil
250g (9oz) carrots, trimmed, peeled
   and cut into quarters lengthways
1 pig's foot cut into half lengthways
   (optional)
salt and black pepper

Unroll the beef and distribute the anchovy fillets over the inside. Pound the spices to powder and sprinkle over. Re-roll and tie again with the seasonings inside.

In a flameproof casserole that will hold the meat snugly cook the bacon until the fat runs. Add the wine and let it boil. Put in the meat, stock, shallots, garlic and bouquet garni and bring to a simmer. Add the carrots and pig's foot, if using. Season with 1 teaspoon salt and some pepper.

Cover tightly with doubled greaseproof paper or foil and the lid of the casserole. Transfer to a low oven, 140°C, 275°F, Gas mark 1, and cook for 4 hours. At the end of the cooking time, remove the meat and vegetables to a warm serving dish. Discard the bouquet garni (and the pig's foot, if used). Skim all the fat off the cooking juices. Serve with a purée of potato and parsnip to soak up the liquid.

If serving cold: remove the beef, allow it to cool, then store in a cold place – it is better not to refrigerate it unless you have no alternative. Strain the cooking juices, then boil to reduce them by one-quarter. Pour into a bowl, chill and lift off the fat when cold. Carve the meat into slices and garnish with the jelly, chopped.

Braised Ox Cheek
with Wine, Cloves and Oranges

Ox cheek is cheap and well flavoured but needs gentle cooking. This recipe also works with braising steak or escalopes if preferred; shorten the cooking time accordingly. In *The Accomplisht Cook* (1685) Robert May gave a recipe for 'stewed collops of beef', which was the inspiration here and an ancestor of all those dishes of steak braised with wine, beer or the highly seasoned sauces made by commercial sauce manufacturers in the 19th century. The key is strong beef stock: use a home-made one if possible, or a good ready-made one, and then reduce it to concentrate the flavour. Really good gravy left from a roast of beef could also be used.

serves
4

600–700g (1lb 5oz–1lb 8oz) ox cheek, cut to give 3–4 thick slices from each one
220ml (8fl oz) red wine
150ml (5fl oz) well-flavoured beef stock

1 orange
6 cloves
scrape of nutmeg
20g (¾oz) flour
20g (¾oz) butter
salt and black pepper

Put the ox cheek in a shallow ovenproof dish. Mix the wine and stock. Remove 4–5 strips of zest from the orange with a canelle knife or a potato peeler and add them, along with the cloves and a generous scrape of nutmeg. Grind in a little black pepper, add about ½ teaspoon salt, and bring the mixture to a simmer. Pour over the beef. Cover tightly with foil and the lid of the dish if it has one. Cook in a low oven, 140°C, 275°F, Gas mark 1 or lower if possible, for 3–3½ hours.

Remove the meat to a warm serving dish. Add the juice of half the orange, or more to taste, plus extra salt and pepper as desired.

Knead the flour and butter together and dot it over the surface of the sauce, shaking the pan so that it melts into the liquid. The sauce may need to be briefly reheated, but don't overdo it – just enough to thicken it lightly. Serve with a very creamy purée of potato, or plain steamed potatoes.

If using braising steak, it can be cooked for a shorter time at a higher temperature – 1½ –2 hours at 150°C, 300°F, Gas mark 2.

Christmas Beef Stew

The inspiration for this was plum pottage, a beef broth made with dried fruit and spices, and laced with alcohol. A tradition at Christmas in 17th- and 18th-century England, it was made in huge quantities and served as a soup. Exactly what this was like isn't obvious – the word pottage (or porridge, as sometimes used) suggests something quite thick, but it may have been thinner, more like a broth or clear soup with a sweet–sour flavour. This version produces something akin to a tagine. If possible, ask the butcher to slice the beef with the bone in.

serves 6

1.5kg (3lb 4oz) shin of beef, in slices
water, to cover
6 cloves
4cm (1½in) piece cinnamon stick
2 teaspoons ground ginger
30g (1oz) sugar
160g (5¼oz) prunes, without stones

60g (2¼oz) raisins
40g (1½oz) currants
zest of ½ orange
zest of 1 lemon
100–150ml (3½–5fl oz) port
juice of 1 lemon
salt

Put the meat in a casserole and just cover with water. Cover and cook in a preheated oven at 140°C, 275°F, Gas mark 1 for 2–2½ hours, by which time the meat should be tender. Drain the liquid into a pan. When the meat is cool enough to handle, pick out the lean meat in nice chunks and set aside. Add the debris and any bones to the stock, and simmer again until the liquid is reduced to about half the original volume. Strain, reserving the liquid. Skim off any fat that rises to the surface.

Put the meat, spices, sugar, dried fruit, and orange and lemon zest into a casserole and add the reserved stock. Heat and then simmer gently – or in a low oven at 160°C, 325°F, Gas mark 3 – for about 1 hour. Add about 1 teaspoon salt, taste, and if it's still on the insipid side, add a little more until the flavour seems about right. Add most of the port and about half the lemon juice. Taste again and adjust with more port, lemon juice or salt as you feel necessary.

Heat gently again until it comes back to the boil and then serve immediately. A good accompaniment is a mixture of potatoes and parsnips, mashed together.

Goulash

A dish that was probably introduced to the British repertoire in the early 20th century. This is based on a version that was regularly made by my mother, who came across it as a child when she lived in Bradford, a city with a significant population of immigrants from Eastern Europe between the world wars. She served it with mashed potatoes or rice, but I prefer pasta.

serves 4

60g (2¼oz) bacon, rinds removed, cut into matchsticks
1 medium onion, peeled and finely sliced
20g (¾oz) lard
1 garlic clove, peeled and crushed
450–500g (1lb–1lb 2oz) stewing beef, trimmed and cut into cubes

1 generous tablespoon paprika
1 teaspoon smoked paprika (optional)
400g (14oz) canned chopped tomatoes
salt
sour cream, to serve

Fry the bacon until the fat runs. Remove it to a casserole and put the onions into the bacon fat. Add a little lard if the bacon hasn't yielded much fat. Let the onions cook very slowly until they are quite soft and beginning to yellow. Add the garlic, cook for a minute or two longer, then drain with a slotted spoon and put to one side with the bacon.

Add any remaining lard, turn up the heat and add the beef. Cook it quite fast, stirring frequently, and when the cubes are browned on all sides, sprinkle in the paprika and the smoked paprika (if using). Cook for a couple of minutes longer, stirring all the time, then add the bacon and onions. Stir in the tomatoes and add a teaspoon of salt. Cover tightly and allow to simmer gently for 1½–2 hours.

At the end of the cooking time, taste and add more salt if desired. Spoon each portion over some buttered noodles or pappardelle and add a spoonful of sour cream to the top. Perhaps not very authentic, but good.

A Welsh Stew

Eliza Acton gave this dish in her book *Modern Cookery for Private Families* (1845). It is recognisably a version of cawl, a soup-like stew of meat and vegetables traditional to Welsh cookery. Acton's version is simple but refined. The better the beef and the stock, the better the end result.

serves
4

about 500g (1lb 2oz) stewing beef, trimmed of any gristle and fat, and cut into slices about 4cm (1½in) square
400ml (14fl oz) beef stock
8 leeks

300g (11oz) small white turnips (or use a slice from a large one)
a pinch sugar
salt and black pepper
chopped parsley, to serve

Put the beef and the stock in a medium-sized flameproof casserole and bring to a simmer. Cover and transfer to a moderate oven, 180°C, 350°F, Gas mark 4. Allow to cook gently for 1 hour.

Prepare the vegetables: cut the white part off the leeks, trim and wash and cut into slices about 2cm (¾in) long (this will probably leave quite a lot of green, the best of which can be used for soup). Peel the turnips: small ones can be cut into quarters; if using a piece of a large one, cut as if making chips.

After 1 hour, remove the casserole from the oven. The beef should be fairly tender and the stock well flavoured. Add the prepared vegetables, 1 teaspoon salt, pepper to taste and a pinch of sugar. Return to the oven for about 1¼ hours. Stir occasionally during this time. Check the seasoning and divide between soup plates.

Dust each portion with parsley and serve with floury potatoes, boiled or steamed.

Ragoût of Oxtail

2 oxtails, cut into pieces
1 medium onion, finely chopped
2 garlic cloves, peeled and crushed
2 bay leaves, spines removed,
   the remainder finely shredded
1 generous tablespoon chopped parsley
leaves of 3–4 sprigs fresh thyme
600ml (1 pint) red wine
200g (7oz) unsmoked pancetta or
   good bacon, cut into dice

250g (9oz) carrot, trimmed, peeled
   and diced
250g (9oz) mushrooms, finely sliced
1 generous tablespoon truffle paste
   (optional)
500g (1lb 2oz) shallots, peeled
450ml (15fl oz) beef stock
40g (1½oz) flour
40g (1½oz) butter
salt and black pepper

Dissolve 1 tablespoon salt in cold water, then soak the oxtail pieces in it for about 1 hour. Drain well. Put the pieces of oxtail into a deep bowl. Mix the chopped onion, garlic, bay leaves, parsley, thyme, a generous quantity of pepper and the wine, and pour over the meat. Cover and leave to marinate for at least 4 hours.

When you're ready to cook the stew, take a large flameproof casserole and set it over a low heat. Add the pancetta or bacon to the casserole and cook until starting to crisp. Put the carrot and mushrooms on top (there's no need to stir), and add the truffle paste, if using. Then add the pieces of meat in a layer, and tuck the shallots into the spaces between.

Pour over the marinade, turn up the heat and let it bubble. Add the beef stock and 1 generous teaspoon salt. Bring to the boil, skim off any scum, and then cover the casserole with foil and the lid, and put in a low oven, 140°C, 275°F, Gas mark 1. Leave strictly alone for 4 hours.

At the end of the cooking time, remove from the oven and skim off as much fat as possible. Taste and correct the seasoning. Knead the flour and butter together to make a *beurre manié* and dot small pieces of this over the surface of the liquid (remove the pieces of oxtail to a hot serving dish if they seem to be in the way). Heat gently and stir until the sauce has thickened.

Serve with mashed potato, or a purée of potato and celeriac.

Lobscouse with Mustard & Parsley Dumplings

Lobscouse is a type of stew that is made around the coasts of north-west Europe, including the port of Liverpool. And yes, that's why Liverpudlians became known as 'scousers'. Beef, fresh or salted, is the most usual principal ingredient, although fish versions are also known. Dumplings are a good, if non-traditional addition. Tender summer carrots, small white turnips and new potatoes are specified for this summer version; winter vegetables, cubed, work equally well but give a more robust flavour.

500g (1lb 2oz) good-quality
  braising steak
200g (7oz) young carrots, trimmed
  and peeled, halved lengthways
200g (7oz) small white turnips, trimmed
  and peeled, and cut into batons
4 garlic cloves, peeled
a bouquet garni of 1 bay leaf, 1 sprig
  rosemary and a few sprigs thyme

300–400ml (10–14fl oz) water
800g (1lb 12oz) new potatoes, scrubbed
salt and black pepper

For the dumplings
1 quantity dumpling mix (see page 26)
1 teaspoon mustard powder
pinch cayenne pepper
1 generous tablespoon chopped parsley

Trim the meat of any obvious fat and gristle, and cut it into 2cm (¾in) cubes. Put the carrots, turnips and the garlic cloves in a layer over the base of a large pan. Tuck the bunch of herbs in among them. Add the beef in a layer on top. Pour in enough water to cover the vegetables and add the salt and some pepper. Cover tightly with a layer of foil under the lid, and put on the lowest heat. Simmer gently for 1 hour, making sure that the liquid doesn't boil away. Then uncover the stew, add the potatoes (cut into halves or quarters if they are large), cover the stew again and continue to cook for about 20 minutes.

Towards the end of cooking, make the dumplings, mixing the mustard, cayenne and parsley into the flour. Uncover the stew, remove the herbs, taste the liquid and add more seasoning if necessary. Drop the dumplings on top of the mixture, re-cover and simmer for another 20 minutes.

Steak and Kidney Pie

Steak and kidney in puddings or pies had become a classic English combination by the early 20th century. Nicely made and carefully seasoned, they remain one of the best dishes in our traditional repertoire. Earlier versions involved pieces of rump steak and kidney, uncooked, enclosed in suet crust and boiled as a pudding. Later ones evolved to be closer to a highly flavoured beef ragoo covered with puff pastry, as described here.

serves 4

40g (1½oz) dripping
1 large onion, chopped
40g (1½oz) flour, plus extra for dusting
500g (1lb 2oz) stewing beef, trimmed
    and cut into 2cm (¾in) cubes
150–200g (5–7oz) ox kidney, trimmed
    and cut into 1cm (½in) cubes

400ml (14fl oz) beef stock
1 bay leaf
½ teaspoon ground allspice
a little Worcestershire sauce
1 quantity puff pastry (see page 25)
beaten egg, cream or milk, to glaze
salt and black pepper

Melt a little of the dripping in a large frying pan and cook the onion gently for about 30 minutes until soft. Remove to a casserole.

Mix the flour with ½ teaspoon salt and some pepper. Toss the steak and kidney in this. Add the rest of the dripping to the frying pan and brown the meat, in batches if necessary, transferring to the casserole when done. Sprinkle any leftover flour into the frying pan to take up the remaining fat and gradually stir in the beef stock, scraping the base of the pan to incorporate all the juices from cooking the meat. Bring to the boil and cook for a few minutes, then pour it over the meat. Add the bay leaf, allspice and a shake of Worcestershire sauce.

Cover, transfer to the oven and cook at 160°C, 325°F, Gas mark 3 for about 2 hours. At the end, taste and add more seasoning as necessary.

Pour into a suitable pie dish and allow to cool. Dust a work surface lightly with flour, roll out the pastry and cover the pie (see page 24). Decorate with leaves made from pastry trimmings, and glaze with egg, cream or milk. Bake at 220°C, 425°F, Gas mark 7 for 20 minutes to raise the pastry, then reduce the heat to 180°C, 350°F, Gas mark 4 for a further 15–20 minutes, or until the filling is reheated thoroughly and piping hot.

Stewed Steak

There are many recipes for stewing or braising steak in English cookery books. They are similar in that they rely on combinations of store-cupboard ingredients – beer, vinegar, and ready-made sauces such as Worcestershire sauce or mushroom ketchup – to produce a strongly flavoured gravy. This is an updated version, which includes a currently fashionable ingredient in the form of balsamic vinegar (but use an inexpensive vinegar, not the costly and precious type). It shares the characteristics of similar recipes from the past, in that it is quick and simple to put together and nice to eat, especially on a cold day.

about 500g (1lb 2oz) braising steak,
    cut into slices about 2cm (¾in) thick
4 garlic cloves, peeled
1 piece of star anise
4 tablespoons soy sauce
2 tablespoons balsamic vinegar
200ml (7fl oz) tomato juice

Put the steak into a shallow ovenproof dish along with the garlic and the star anise. Mix together the other ingredients and pour over. Cover the dish with foil and then with a lid if the dish has one. Cook in a low oven, 140°C, 275°F, Gas mark 1, for 3 hours, by which time the meat should be extremely tender and surrounded by a well-flavoured sauce. Serve hot with a mixture of potato and parsnip mashed together.

Veal and Ham Pie

serves
4–6

400–500g (14oz–1lb 2oz) veal,
  preferably from the loin or leg
100–150g (3½–5oz) cooked ham in
  one piece
2 hard-boiled eggs
1 generous tablespoon chopped parsley
leaves from a few sprigs winter
  savoury or thyme, chopped
15–20 large leaves of fresh basil,
  torn into pieces
2 bay leaves, spines removed and
  the leaves shredded
pinch cinnamon
120ml (4fl oz) well-reduced
  stock – veal for preference,
  otherwise chicken

salt and black pepper
1 quantity puff pastry (see page 25)
flour, for dusting
beaten egg, cream or milk,
  to glaze

For the forcemeat
200g (7oz) spinach, well washed
200g (7oz) breadcrumbs made
  with fresh white bread
50g (2oz) fat bacon (unsmoked),
  cut into small pieces
½ teaspoon salt
1 egg

Cut the veal, ham and hard-boiled eggs into thin slices. Mix together the parsley, winter savoury or thyme leaves, half the basil leaves and the bay leaves. Add the cinnamon, salt and pepper. Toss the veal pieces in this and put on one side.

Put the spinach in a pan; the only water it will need is that left on the leaves from washing it. Put it over medium heat with a lid on. Stir until wilted, then tip it into a sieve and press well to remove excess water. Put it together with the breadcrumbs, bacon, remaining basil leaves and salt into a liquidiser or food processor, then blend to a paste. Add the egg and process just enough to mix.

Take a deep pie dish and put a layer of ham in the base. Cover this with some of the forcemeat. Add the slices of hard-boiled egg, then more forcemeat, then the veal, interspersed with any remaining forcemeat. Pour in the stock.

Roll out the pastry and cover the dish (see page 24). Glaze with beaten egg, cream or milk. Cook at 220°C, 425°F, Gas mark 7 for 20 minutes, reduce to 180°C, 350°F, Gas mark 4 and cook for a further 45 minutes to 1 hour.

Roast Veal with Sorrel Purée

A traditional combination lovely for a meal in late spring. Sorrel is not easy to obtain, but it is worth growing it or trying to buy some because it makes a delicious accompaniment for many things besides veal. For sorrel purée the relative amounts of sorrel and cream are fairly flexible.

serves 6

a piece of veal for roasting
  (topside, loin or chump)
  about 1.5–2kg (3½lb–4½lb)
30g (1oz) unsalted butter
1 scant teaspoon lemon zest
  (preferably unwaxed),
  finely grated
½ teaspoon black peppercorns,
  coarsely ground

1 fresh bay leaf – discard the central
  spine, and shred the leaf finely
salt

For the sorrel purée
15g (½oz) unsalted butter
100g (4oz) sorrel, washed and picked
  over – remove any tough stalks
150ml (5fl oz) double cream
salt and pepper

An hour or two before you want to cook the veal, soften the butter and mix in the lemon zest, pepper and bay leaf. Rub this mixture all over the meat and leave it, covered, in a cool place.

For cooking, select a roasting tin or casserole into which the meat will fit neatly, without too much space round the edges. Do not cover. Preheat the oven to 190°C, 375°F, Gas mark 5. Cook for 15–20 minutes, then reduce the heat to 180°C, 350°F, Gas mark 4 and continue to cook, basting with the juices from time to time. Salt lightly towards the end of cooking, and rest for 15 minutes.

Just before serving, make the sorrel purée. Melt the butter in a saucepan and add the sorrel, still damp but not wringing wet from washing, then stir over a gentle heat until it collapses. The colour will change from a vivid green to a less attractive grey-brown, but don't let this worry you. As soon as it is all cooked, remove from the heat. Pour the cream into a clean pan and bring to the boil. Add the sorrel and cook gently for 2 minutes; add seasoning to taste.

Carve the meat in thin slices and spoon some of the buttery cooking juices over each plate. Serve with new potatoes and the sorrel purée.

Veal with Orange and Verjuice

The original idea for this came from a book first published in France by an author known simply as La Varenne. Translated into English as *The French Cook* (1653), it was an important text in the development of cookery techniques. This recipe uses verjuice (the juice of unripe apples or grapes), and it gives a pleasant fruity sourness without being overwhelming. If you can't get verjuice, use a not-too-dry white wine in this recipe.

serves 6

a piece of veal topside, about
    1.5kg (3½lb)
40g (1½oz) unsalted butter, softened
about 200ml (7fl oz) stock, preferably
    veal or chicken
about 1 tablespoon plain flour
salt

For the marinade
zest of 1 orange (preferably
    unwaxed), in thin strips
zest of ½ lemon (preferably
    unwaxed), in thin strips
6 tablespoons verjuice or wine
freshly ground black pepper

For the marinade, mix the orange and lemon zests with the verjuice and a little freshly ground pepper. Turn the veal in this mixture and leave to marinate for 5–6 hours, or overnight.

When you want to cook the meat, remove it from the marinade and scrape any bits of zest back into the marinade mixture.

Spread the butter over the meat, add a little salt, and put the meat in a roasting tin into which it fits reasonably well. Strain in the liquid from the marinade. Cook at 190°C, 375°F, Gas mark 5 for 15 minutes, then reduce the heat to 180°C, 350°F, Gas mark 4 and allow 25–30 minutes per 500g, basting frequently and adding a little stock to the tin if the juices show signs of drying up. About 15 minutes before the end of cooking time, add the zest from the marinade to the roasting tin (do not add it any earlier, or it will burn and blacken).

When the meat is done, remove it to a warmed serving dish and allow to rest. Pour the juices from the tin into a bowl. Deglaze the tin with a little stock, then add this to the juices. Spoon off excess fat, returning about 1 tablespoon of the liquid to the roasting tin, and sprinkle in a little flour. Stir over a low heat until it browns slightly, then stir in the cooking juices to make gravy.

Veal Olives

These thinly rolled slices of veal were often used as pie fillings in the 17th and 18th centuries, but they are very good on their own with a little sauce. The name has nothing to do with olives but is derived from an old French word for lark: the little meat rolls, plumply stuffed, are reminiscent of small birds lying in the dish.

Mace, a popular spice in the 18th century, is best bought whole; crush it to a powder with a mortar and pestle just before using. The recipe can be used with beef olives as well – omit the Parma ham and use red wine and beef stock as the cooking liquids.

serves
4

4 veal escalopes, each weighing
    approximately 100g (3½oz)
2 slices Parma ham
100g (3½oz) breadcrumbs
50g (2oz) butter, plus a little extra
    for frying
2 anchovies
leaves of 3–4 sprigs thyme

zest of ½ lemon, finely grated
about ½ teaspoon ground mace
1 small egg
200g (7oz) button mushrooms,
    trimmed and sliced
120ml (4fl oz) dry sherry
120ml (4fl oz) veal or chicken stock
salt and black pepper

Lay the escalopes on a plate or board and cover each one with a slice of Parma ham. Put the breadcrumbs in a bowl. Melt the butter and crush the anchovies into it. Pour into the breadcrumbs, add the thyme, lemon, mace and some black pepper. Mix in the egg, stir well, divide into four and spread each portion over the ham on top of the escalopes. Roll up, enclosing the stuffing, and tie each olive with thread in two or three places.

Melt a little butter and fry the olives briefly, just enough to brown lightly. Remove to a plate, and add the sliced mushrooms to the pan. Fry over fairly high heat, stirring well until they brown a little. Put the rolls of meat back in, pour in the sherry and let it bubble, then add the stock. Bring to a simmer, cover and transfer to a moderate oven, 150°C, 300°F, Gas mark 2 for 1 hour.

Serve with plain boiled rice.

Spring Stew of Veal

In summer, English cooks liked to pair veal with fresh greenery and slightly acid flavours. Sorrel was often chosen, but this more unusual combination of cucumbers, gooseberries and lettuce was suggested by Eliza Acton in 1845. She cooked everything together from the start, but the vegetables become very soft this way. Put them in about halfway through cooking, so that they retain a little texture.

serves 4

450–500g (1lb–1lb 2oz) stewing veal, cut into 2cm (¾in) cubes
30g (1oz) flour
40g (1½oz) butter
6 spring onions, trimmed, washed and cut into 2cm (¾in) lengths
150g (5oz) green gooseberries
350ml (12fl oz) veal or chicken stock

½ cucumber, peeled, seeds removed and the flesh cut into 1cm (½in) dice
2 Little Gem lettuces, outer leaves removed, trimmed, washed and cut into quarters lengthways
salt and black pepper
chives, to garnish

Toss the veal in the flour. Melt the butter in a frying pan or flameproof casserole. Add the veal and fry briskly to brown. Add the spring onions and gooseberries and continue to fry for a few minutes. Stir in any remaining flour, then add the stock, stirring well to make a sauce. Add ½ teaspoon salt and a little pepper. Cover well and simmer gently for about 1 hour, stirring occasionally.

Add the cucumber and lettuce. Cover and cook for a further 1 hour, or until the meat is tender and the vegetables cooked. Stir, check the seasoning, and garnish with a scatter of chopped chives. Serve with new potatoes.

Lamb and Mutton

LAMB AND MUTTON both refer to the meat of sheep, but there is an age distinction and, unless you are a shepherd or a butcher, the terminology can be confusing. Alive, a sheep is considered a lamb from birth in the spring until the turn of the year. For the next 12 months, the animal becomes a hoggett, and after that it is a sheep. As meat, lambs may be killed at about 10–12 weeks old for Easter, but most reach the market at between 5 and 12 months. Then it enters a kind of culinary no man's land, when it is really mutton, but mutton that is too young to have acquired flavour or character. After its second winter, the meat will taste more interesting, especially if grazed on some distinctive species-rich grassland or hill pasture. The full flavour develops at around 3 years old, but to be really good, the best mutton came from animals 5 or even 6 years old.

Cooking lamb in stews and pies

Most sheep meat that arrives on the market is described as lamb, a convention I've followed here, although the animals concerned are often well on their way to adulthood. Mutton is difficult to buy and generally comes from ewes. It is impossible to find the mutton known in the past. The fine distinctions once made between these meats are no longer available to us.

All lamb is relatively tender. Even cuts that appear lean, such as leg, can be cut up for stews, but they are expensive and are more usually used for roasting. 'Stewing lamb' usually indicates meat from the neck – best end, middle or scrag. Best end is most elegant and is relatively expensive, as it often gets used as a rack of lamb for roasting. Middle and scrag are less easy to find than previously. Scrag may seem unpromising, containing a lot of bone and fat, but like all neck of lamb cuts, it has an excellent flavour. It also produces good stock as it cooks, something on which the homely mutton and potato dishes depend. Shoulder of lamb, usually sold in the past as a whole or a half for roasting, can be found as smaller pieces, as steaks or sometimes as 'henrys' (quarters), good for using in stews. If desired, the meat can be cut off the bones. Lamb shanks, usually cut from the leg, but sometimes from the shoulder, are excellent for stewing.

Cuts such as neck and shanks must be cooked very slowly for about 3 hours, allowing the large amounts of collagen they contain to soften and gelatinise, adding body to the dish so that the flavours develop and permeate sauces. Potatoes absorb some of the fat contained in the meat. Shoulder steaks and better-quality lamb, diced, can be cooked on higher temperatures for shorter times (about 1½ hours in a moderate oven).

The distinctive and strong flavour of lamb responds well to many treatments. Root vegetables, especially onions, carrots and turnips, make a good basic stew in the style used for simple beef casseroles. Flavours from maritime environments are also excellent.

Buying lamb and mutton and cuts for roasting

Butchers often identify where their lamb comes from. The ideal supplier will know the farmers who rear the animals and will be able to tell you about the produce. Lamb should hang for 7–10 days. Mutton can hang for longer; 19th-century cooks thought it should hang for as long as possible. Look for firm, dull red lean meat in lamb and dull brownish-red in mutton, with hard white fat and small bones. Avoid excessive fat. Mutton can be difficult to buy but a good butcher may be able to source it.

Sheep are cut into fore- and hindquarters. The hindquarter includes the leg, a favourite roasting joint that weighs 2–3.5kg (4½–7¾lb), depending on the breed and age of the animal. It is usually possible to buy a half leg, which means you have to choose between a round piece of lean, or a longer, slimmer shank end, with smaller muscles, but sweeter meat. The loin (which together with the leg makes a haunch) is also a good roasting joint, but since it is usually cut into chops, this has to be ordered. Equally, you are unlikely to be able to buy a haunch except by special request.

The forequarter includes the 'best end', or rack of lamb. This is a very good small roasting joint, with a neat appearance when nicely trimmed; make sure it is chined and that the long bones are divided at the joints to make it easy to separate them. The shoulder contains the bladebone and the long bone adjoining it, plus a knuckle. Bonier and fattier than leg, it is a good roasting joint with a sweeter flavour, and is cheaper. A whole shoulder will generally weigh 2–2.5kg (4½–5½lb), up to 3–3.5kg (6½–7¾lb) for mutton, but it is often sold cut diagonally in half. Finally, the breast – a cut taken from the ends of the ribs – can also be used for roasting. It tends to be chewy, as it contains thin sheets of muscle interspersed with connective tissue, and is also fatty, but has a good flavour and is very inexpensive.

As with beef, how long you cook your lamb (rare or well done) is down to personal preference. For people who are undecided, leg and best end are probably better cooked on the rare side, but shoulder benefits from being fully cooked – this will cook out some of the fat and crisp up the skin.

For individual recipes, I have given specific temperatures and approximate times, but if all you want is a plain roast joint of lamb or mutton, times and temperatures for fast roasting are similar to those for beef, although I would start it at a slightly lower temperature:

• For a fast roast, give the meat 20 minutes at 220°C, 425°F, Gas mark 7, then reduce the heat to 180°C, 350°F, Gas mark 4 and cook for the following times:
   Lamb or mutton on the bone: 15 minutes per 500g (rare); 18–20 minutes per 500g (medium); 25 minutes per 500g (well done). Boneless: 12 minutes per 500g (rare); 13–15 minutes per 500g (medium); 20 minutes per 500g (well done).

• For slow roasting, which works well with leg of mutton, cook at 150°C, 300°F, Gas mark 2 for the entire time, allowing 60 minutes per 500g.

• For breast of lamb or mutton, see the recipe on page 82.

Rack of Lamb with a Herb Crust

The rack, or best end of neck of lamb, consists of 6–8 cutlets joined together, and must be chined. Often the ends of the bones are cleaned of all meat, and sometimes decorated with paper frills. Two racks presented with the bones making a crisscross formation are known as a guard of honour; three, curved and stitched together vertically so that the meat is inside and the bones radiate in a sunburst, is a crown roast, which was very fashionable during the 1970s. A lone rack of lamb is a good joint for 2–3 people (although don't expect leftovers), and also one that is nice cold; the coating of breadcrumbs recalls 17th- and 18th-century 'dredges' of flavoured crumbs.

serves 2–3

1 rack of lamb, trimmed
1 fresh rosemary sprig
30g (1oz) fresh white breadcrumbs
2 tablespoons chopped parsley
1 tablespoon chopped basil
1 garlic clove, peeled and crushed
½ teaspoon salt

Preheat the oven to 180°C, 350°F, Gas mark 4.

Remove the parchment-like skin covering the meat (a thin layer of fat should remain) and scrape the bones if the butcher hasn't done this for you. Put the lamb, bones down, in a small roasting tin or ovenproof dish, tucking in the rosemary underneath. Roast for 30–40 minutes, depending on the size.

While the lamb cooks, mix the breadcrumbs, parsley, basil, garlic and salt. After the initial roasting, remove the meat from the oven and turn up the heat to 200°C, 400°F, Gas mark 6. Carefully spread the breadcrumb and herb mixture over the fat layer, pressing it down well. Roast for another 10 minutes.

This roast does not produce any gravy worth speaking of, so if you're serving it hot, good accompaniments are ones that add moisture or a dish of baked tomatoes.

Breast of Lamb Stuffed with Capers, Garlic and Herbs

serves 3–4

2 breasts of lamb, boned
40g (1½oz) unsalted butter
1 medium onion, peeled and finely
    chopped
2 garlic cloves, peeled and crushed
2 tablespoons salted capers, well rinsed
    and coarsely chopped
a little chopped fresh mint

3 tablespoons finely chopped fresh
    parsley
large tablespoon chopped fresh basil
zest of ½ lemon (preferably unwaxed),
    finely grated
150g (5oz) crustless day-old white
    bread, torn into small pieces
splash of stock or milk, to moisten

Breast of lamb is flattish and thin, with one straight edge cut from the forequarter, which may still contain the ends of the rib bones, unless the butcher has removed them. To do this yourself, run a knife in between the bones and the meat on the outside, then cut them away from the lesser covering inside and slip them out.

To make the stuffing, melt the butter over a low heat and fry the onion and garlic until softened. Stir in the capers, herbs, lemon zest and bread, and add enough stock or milk to moisten the bread.

Spread the meat out, skin-side down. Put a layer of stuffing on top of each piece, then roll from the narrow end and tie at each end with string – firmly, but not so tight that all the stuffing oozes out.

Preheat the oven to 140°C, 275°F, Gas mark 1. Put the lamb in a shallow roasting tin and cook for 3–3½ hours, pouring off any fat. Then turn the oven up to 200°C, 400°F, Gas mark 6, and give it a further 15 minutes to crisp up.

It will not produce gravy, but a light tomato sauce goes well with the caper-flavoured stuffing. Alternatively, serve a salad dressed with vinaigrette on the side.

Irish Stew

Comfort food. A simple, inexpensive dish known in the cookery of Ireland and Britain since at least the mid-19th century. Irish Stew was originally made in a pan, cooked gently on top of the stove, and often considered better if some of the potatoes began to dissolve into the mixture, thickening it. The best stews were said to be made with the minimum of water or stock. Cooking in the oven means it can be left to look after itself – but put it in a pan and simmer on the very lowest heat on the hob if preferred. It has a gentle, mild flavour; if you find it bland, try adding the mixture suggested at the end.

serves 4

300g (11oz) onion, peeled and coarsely chopped

1kg (2lb 4oz) neck of lamb (middle or scrag), cut into chops

300g (11oz) small white turnips, trimmed, peeled, halved and cut into slices lengthways

1.2kg (2lb 11oz) potatoes, peeled and cut into large dice

salt and black pepper

300ml (10fl oz) stock (lamb for preference)

To garnish (optional)

a handful of fresh coriander leaves

1 small garlic clove, peeled

1 fresh hot green chilli, to taste

a little finely grated lemon zest

Take a large casserole (or pan) and build the meat and vegetables in layers, beginning with the onion and following with the meat, turnips and potatoes, then repeating until the ingredients are used up. Sprinkle on 1 teaspoon of salt and some pepper between the layers. Bring the stock to the boil, pour over the meat and vegetables and cover with buttered foil or paper and the lid.

Cook in the oven, 180°C, 350°F, Gas mark 4, for at least 2 hours, or longer on a lower temperature, if desired. A stew simmering on the hob will need checking occasionally to make sure it isn't drying out.

At the end of cooking, taste, correct the seasoning, and serve straight from the pot. To garnish, chop the coriander leaves, garlic and green chilli fairly finely, stir in the lemon zest and scatter a little of this mixture over each portion.

Braised Lamb Shanks

Lamb shanks usually remained attached to roasts of lamb until the early 1980s, at which point a change in fashion liberated them to become foundations for dishes in their own right. Slowly cooked in rich, savoury sauces, they have become a modern British classic.

serves 4

4 lamb shanks
2 tablespoons olive oil, plus extra
    for frying
300ml (10fl oz) red wine
salt and black pepper
1 medium–large onion, peeled
    and chopped finely
2 garlic cloves, peeled and
    chopped finely

the leaves from 1 sprig rosemary,
    peeled and chopped finely
1 generous tablespoon flour
a bouquet garni of a few sprigs
    each of parsley, marjoram,
    mint and basil plus 2 strips
    of orange zest
about 150ml (5fl oz) lamb or
    beef stock

Put the lamb shanks in a suitable bowl and add the oil, wine, 1 teaspoon salt and some pepper. Cover and leave the meat in the marinade for at least 2 hours (overnight is better). Turn the meat in the mixture occasionally. When ready to cook, drain the meat from the marinade, reserving the marinade for the sauce.

Heat a little olive oil in a flameproof casserole. Add the onion, garlic and rosemary and fry briskly, stirring frequently, until it is just beginning to turn golden. Pat the meat dry, toss it in the flour and add to the mixture, turning well until lightly browned. Dust in any remaining flour. Pour in the marinade, stir well and bring to the boil, stirring well. Add the bouquet garni and the stock and return the mixture to the boil.

Cover the pot with foil and then with the lid. Cook in a preheated oven at 150°C, 300°F, Gas mark 2 for 2½–3 hours. At the end of cooking time, taste the sauce and add more seasoning if necessary. Serve with mashed or jacket potatoes.

Lamb Stewed with Samphire, Capers and Artichokes

Recipes using flavours derived from maritime environments appear in cookery books from the 17th century onwards. Here is one inspired by dishes mentioned by Jos Cooper in *The Art of Cookery Refin'd and Augmented* (1654) and Robert May in *The Accomplisht Cook* (1685). Use mutton if it is available: this was a dish for meat with depth of flavour. Samphire is a plant with fleshy, brilliant green stems. It grows on salt marshes, which are often used for grazing sheep, and is available from fishmongers from late May until September. It is a winter food and habitat for certain birds, so always check that it is sustainably harvested.

Fresh artichokes can be used if available: buy four, trim away the tops of the leaves, remove the thistly choke from the centre and boil for a few minutes until tender, then add them to the stew.

serves
4

2 tablespoons olive oil
1 small onion, peeled and finely chopped
1 garlic clove, peeled and crushed
about 750g (1lb 10oz) lamb or
    mutton chops, loin, chump
    or best end of neck
1 tablespoon flour
100ml (3½fl oz) red wine
1 anchovy, either salted or preserved in oil

150ml (5fl oz) beef stock or water
a little nutmeg
100g (3½oz) samphire
30g (1oz) salted capers
100–125g (3½–4½oz) globe artichokes
    preserved in oil – drained weight
salt and black pepper
chopped parsley, to serve

Heat 1 tablespoon olive oil in a frying pan or flameproof casserole and add the onion and garlic. Cook gently, stirring frequently, until soft and golden. Remove with a slotted spoon.

Trim any excess fat off the chops, then coat lightly with the flour. Add the remaining olive oil to the pan and fry them on either side until lightly browned, then sprinkle in any remaining flour and stir well. Still stirring, add the wine and let it come to the boil, then add the anchovy and stock or water. Mix well and bring to a simmer. Grate in a little nutmeg and add a couple of turns of black pepper. Cover and simmer very gently or put the casserole in a moderate oven, 180°C, 350°F, Gas mark 4, for about 45 minutes, or until the meat is tender.

Rinse the samphire and pick it over, discarding any soft or discoloured bits. Rinse the capers free from salt, and drain any oil from the artichokes. Cut them into quarters if this has not already been done.

When the meat is cooked, skim off any excess fat. Add the samphire, capers and artichokes to the stew, stir gently, and return to the oven for 5–10 minutes, just long enough for the samphire to cook and the capers and artichokes to heat through. Taste and add salt if necessary, but this is unlikely because the capers and anchovy will provide plenty.

Dust with parsley and serve with new potatoes.

Lamb Korma

This recipe was written by Colonel Kenny-Herbert in the late 19th century in his book *Culinary Jottings for Madras* (1885). This 'quoorma', as he spelt it, is a reminder that curry in the 19th century was not always a mixture of cold meat re-hashed with a stock curry powder. I make no apology for lifting his recipe almost exactly as he detailed it because it is excellent, but have halved the quantity of butter – the 4oz (120g) originally suggested seemed a little too much.

serves 4–6

about 700g (1lb 8oz) leg of lamb, fillet end for preference
50g (2oz) fresh root ginger, peeled and grated
1 teaspoon salt
50g (2oz) butter
2 medium onions, peeled and sliced
2 garlic cloves, peeled and finely chopped

spice mixture – made from 1 teaspoon coriander seed, 1 teaspoon black peppercorns, ½ teaspoon cloves and ½ teaspoon cardamom seeds ground together
150ml (5fl oz) single cream
100g (3½oz) almonds, blanched
1 dessertspoon turmeric
1 teaspoon sugar
the juice of 2 limes

Cut the meat into neat pieces about 2cm (¾in) square, discarding any bone and fat. Put the pieces in a bowl with the grated ginger and salt, then stir well and leave to marinate in a cool place for about 2 hours.

Melt the butter in a heavy flameproof casserole. Add the onions and garlic and cook gently until they begin to turn light gold – this will take about 30 minutes. Then add the meat mixture and fry, turning frequently, until well browned.

Stir in the spice mixture and continue to cook gently for a few minutes. Warm the cream to almost boiling and put it with the almonds into a blender. Whizz together to reduce the almonds to fragments, then press through a sieve; use a little water to help the process if the mixture is very thick. Stir the almond-flavoured cream into the meat along with the turmeric and sugar, then place over the lowest possible heat and cook very gently for about 40 minutes. Stir frequently, making sure it doesn't stick. Add a little water as necessary. Check to make sure the meat is cooked through, then stir in the lime juice.

Harrico of Mutton or Lamb

The word haricot (or harrico) is derived from French *harigoter*, meaning 'to cut up'. It meant a stew or ragoo, but got confused with the usage of haricot as a name for beans in French, and sometimes led English cooks to think that haricot of mutton included beans. This summery version doesn't, but by all means add some fresh French beans towards the end of cooking time.

This recipe is based on one given by Anne Cobbett in her book *The English Housekeeper* (1851). She evidently considered the basic recipe bland and added proprietary sauces popular in the mid-19th century. I've suggested Thai fish sauce, which adds a salty note. For the stock, use lamb or chicken stock, simmered with turnip, carrot, onion and parsley to strengthen the flavour.

serves 4

500–600g (1lb 2oz–1lb 5oz) lamb or mutton – best end of neck, loin or chump chops
30g (1oz) butter
400ml (14fl oz) strong stock
4–6 small young carrots, trimmed, peeled and cut into quarters lengthways
a bunch of spring onions, washed, trimmed, and cut into 3–4cm (1¼–1½in) lengths

200g (7oz) small white turnips or kohlrabi, peeled and cut into sticks
4 celery sticks cut into 3–4cm (1¼–1½in) lengths
15g (½oz) flour
salt and black pepper

To season (optional)
cayenne pepper
Worcestershire sauce
Nam pla (Thai fish sauce)

Trim the chops of any excessive fat. Melt half the butter – around 15g (½ oz) – in a large frying pan and brown the chops on both sides. Add the stock, bring to the boil and simmer gently for 45 minutes. Add the vegetables and continue to cook gently for another 15–20 minutes. By this time, the meat should be tender. Season carefully. A pinch of cayenne, following Anne Cobbett's example, is a good addition, as are about 1 teaspoon of each of the sauces. If using these, remember that they are salty, and add them before finally tasting and adding any more salt and pepper.

Knead the remaining butter with the flour and drop into the stew in small pieces. Heat gently until boiling, shaking to distribute the butter through the liquid so that the sauce thickens. Serve with new potatoes, and other vegetables as desired.

Lamb Meatballs

Recipes for meatballs appear in early English recipe books from the end of the 16th century until the middle of the 18th century. They were highly seasoned and enhanced with whatever spices, dried fruit and nuts happened to be fashionable at the time. This version is loosely based on recipes from the early 18th century.

serves
4

400g (14oz) minced lamb
50g (2oz) fresh white breadcrumbs
1 garlic clove, peeled and crushed
1 tablespoon very finely chopped
    parsley
1 tablespoon finely chopped basil
½ teaspoon nutmeg
1 egg
30g (1oz) pistachio nuts, blanched
    (optional)

2 rashers fatty bacon (unsmoked),
    diced
10–12 small shallots, peeled
150ml (5fl oz) red wine
150ml (5fl oz) good stock,
    beef for preference
2 teaspoons cornflour, slaked
    with a little water
salt and black pepper

Put the lamb, breadcrumbs, garlic, herbs, nutmeg, 1 teaspoon salt, pepper to taste, and the egg into a large bowl. Mix well, a task best done by kneading all together by hand.

Divide the mixture into 20, and form each piece into a small ball (wet your hands in cold water to stop it sticking). If using pistachio nuts, seal one or two in the centre of each little ball. Heat a deep frying pan or shallow flameproof casserole and add the bacon pieces. Fry gently until they have yielded most of their fat. Add the peeled shallots and the meatballs and let them cook gently, turning occasionally until the meatballs have browned on all sides.

Pour in the wine and let it bubble, then add the stock. Cover and cook gently for 30–45 minutes. Then stir in the cornflour mixture, heating gently and stirring all the time until the sauce thickens. Taste and correct the seasoning if necessary. Serve with plain boiled rice or mashed potato and a salad of bitter leaves.

Bolton Hotpot

oysters – as many as you like or can
   afford, up to 20 (optional)
50g (2oz) beef dripping
1 large onion, peeled and thinly sliced
2 garlic cloves, peeled and crushed
800g–1kg (1lb 12oz–2lb 4oz) middle
   neck of lamb, cut into chops
30g (1oz) flour
400ml (14fl oz) stock, preferably lamb

2 lamb's kidneys, cored and
   cut into slices
pinch ground allspice
250g (9oz) mushrooms, sliced
   fairly thinly
900g (2lb) potatoes, peeled
   and sliced
a little butter
salt and black pepper

If using oysters, open them first, or ask the fishmonger to do so. Strain and reserve any liquor they contain to remove stray bits of shell or grit.

Melt the dripping in a frying pan and add the onion. Cook fairly briskly until it is starting to yellow. Add the garlic, stir well, cook for a moment longer, then drain and remove the onions to a large deep casserole or other ovenproof dish. Put the chops into the hot fat and brown on both sides, then put these on top of the onions.

Sprinkle the flour into the fat left in the pan and stir to make a roux. Stir in the heated stock to make a sauce. Add 1 generous teaspoon salt and plenty of pepper. Allow it to cook gently for a few minutes. Put the kidneys on top of the chops and dust them with a little allspice. Follow this with the sliced mushrooms in a layer, then the oysters, if you are using them. Add the oyster liquor if there is any, and pour over the sauce from the frying pan. Put the potatoes on top, ending with a nice neat layer of large overlapping slices. Dot with small pieces of butter.

Cover with the lid of the casserole and cook at 180°C, 350°F, Gas mark 4 for about 2½ hours. Then uncover the pot and turn the heat up to 200°C, 400°F, Gas mark 6, and cook for another 20 minutes to brown the potatoes.

Pickled red cabbage is the traditional accompaniment to hotpot in Lancashire.

Scotch Broth

Stock from lamb or mutton bones has a distinctive flavour, best used with robust vegetable combinations found in the Scotch Broth tradition.

serves
4

1 litre (1¾ pints) stock made with the
   bones from a lamb or mutton roast
40g (1½oz) split peas (yellow or green),
   soaked overnight
40g (1½oz) pearl barley
2 medium carrots, scraped and sliced
1 small turnip, about 75g (3oz), peeled
   and chopped
1 leek, cleaned, trimmed and chopped

1 celery stick, washed and chopped
a few leaves of curly kale, washed and
   shredded
salt and pepper
chopped parsley

Put the stock in a pan and add the soaked split peas, barley and all the vegetables except the kale. Simmer gently until the peas and barley are soft. Add the kale and cook for about 10 minutes longer. Check the seasoning and add salt and pepper as needed.

Divide the broth between bowls and add parsley just before serving.

Indian Shepherd's Pie

serves
4

3 tablespoons oil

3 cloves

3 cardamom pods

1 large onion, peeled and very finely
chopped

4 garlic cloves, peeled and crushed

2cm (¾in) cube of fresh root ginger,
peeled and grated

1 teaspoon cumin seed, toasted in a
warm frying pan and then ground

1 teaspoon coriander seeds, ground

½ teaspoon turmeric

pinch chilli pepper, or to taste

450–500g (1lb–1lb 2oz) minced lamb

2 large tomatoes, peeled and chopped

100ml (3½fl oz) water

½–1 teaspoon garam masala

salt and black pepper

1 tablespoon chopped mint

For the topping

900g (2lb) potatoes, peeled
and cut into chunks

100ml (3½fl oz) milk

40g (1½oz) butter

2 tablespoons chopped
coriander leaves

1 fresh mild green chilli,
finely chopped

chilli powder or hot fresh chilli
(finely chopped), to taste

salt and black pepper

Heat the oil in a large frying pan. Add the cloves and cardamom and allow them to heat through, then add the onion. Fry gently, stirring frequently, until it is beginning to brown evenly – this will take at least 20 minutes.

Add the garlic and ginger and continue to cook for 1–2 minutes, then add the cumin, coriander and turmeric, plus a pinch of chilli pepper. Stir well to heat the spices, then add the minced lamb. Keep stirring it and breaking up any lumps until the meat is lightly browned and the onion mixture is well amalgamated with it. Add the tomatoes and the water, then turn the heat down low, cover, and allow the mixture to simmer for a minimum of 1 hour, or 2 hours if possible. Stir from time to time and add a little water if it shows signs of drying out. At the end of cooking time, stir in the garam masala, salt to taste and the mint. Pour the mixture into an ovenproof dish, then remove the cloves and the cardamom pods.

To make the topping, boil the potatoes, drain and mash with the milk and butter, adding salt to taste and quite a lot of black pepper. Stir in the coriander leaves and the mild chilli; add a little chilli powder or hot chilli to taste.

Spread the mashed potato over the meat mixture, roughening the surface with a fork. Bake in the oven at 190°C, 375°F, Gas mark 5 for about 25–30 minutes, or until the potato is browning, or chill and reheat later, allowing about 40–45 minutes and making sure the pie is properly heated through.

Slow-Roast Mutton and Salsa Verde

This recipe was originally created for Herdwick mutton; these sheep, born with black pelts that turn grey or rusty brown as they grow, have distinctive pale heads, small curved horns, and are principally found on the highest of the Lake District fells. Meat from other breeds will work equally well, although try to acquire mutton rather than lamb. Salsa verde, which includes both capers and mint, recalls the English traditions of caper sauce with mutton and mint sauce with lamb.

serves 6–8

a whole leg of mutton, bone in salt

For the salsa verde
a good handful each of fresh mint,
    parsley and basil
1 small garlic clove, peeled and
    crushed
2 tablespoons capers, rinsed of any salt
    or vinegar in which they have been
    preserved
2 tablespoons Dijon mustard
2 tablespoons red wine vinegar
8 tablespoons olive oil

Salt the meat lightly and cook in a very low oven, 140°C, 275°F, Gas mark 1, allowing 60 minutes per 500g.

To make the salsa verde, wash the herbs and pick off the leaves, discarding the stalks. Blend all the ingredients together, taste and season.

Carve the roast mutton and serve the sauce separately.

Roast Leg of Mutton with Anchovies and Orange Peel

serves
8

3kg (6½lb) leg of mutton, bone in
1 tablespoon olive oil
2 large garlic cloves, peeled and each
 cut into 2–3 chunks
1 large shallot, peeled and quartered
1 bay leaf (optional)
some fresh marjoram sprigs (optional)
200ml (7fl oz) red wine
200ml (7fl oz) well-flavoured stock
2 tablespoons plain flour

freshly ground black pepper
½ teaspoon salt

For the larding
8–10 anchovy fillets preserved in oil,
 drained
1 large orange (preferably unwaxed)
18–20 fresh rosemary sprigs,
 about 3cm (1¼in) long

Cut the anchovy fillets into strips about 2cm (¾in) long and 5mm (¼in) wide. Pare the zest from the orange to make about 20–25 strips of zest. Keep the orange – you'll need the juice later.

Take the mutton and use a sharp knife to make parallel rows of small incisions, about 4cm (1½in) apart, from the broad end to the shank. Make a row, with rosemary sprigs in each incision; in the second row, pieces of anchovy; in the third row, slivers of orange zest. Repeat until the larding ingredients have been used up.

Put the olive oil in a roasting tin. Add the garlic and shallot, the bay leaf and the marjoram. Sit the meat on top and sprinkle with salt. Cook at 170°C, 325°F, Gas mark 3 for about 2 hours, then pour the red wine and the juice of the orange into the roasting tin and return to roast for a further 1½ hours, until the juices run clear. Put the joint on a warm plate, cover loosely with foil, and leave to rest.

Pour the cooking juices into a bowl. Put the roasting tin over a low heat. Stir in half the stock, scraping the tin to incorporate all the residue, and add to the reserved juices. Return the tin to the heat and add 2–3 tablespoons of the meat fat. Stir in the flour and allow to brown lightly, but not burn. Skim any fat off the cooking juices. Strain these into the tin, stirring, and bring to the boil to make a lightly thickened gravy. Add the remainder of the stock, taste, and check the seasoning.

Shoulder of Mutton with or without Oysters

serves
6

1 shoulder of mutton, 2–2.5kg
    (4½–5½lb), boned weight
1 tablespoon finely chopped fresh
    marjoram
zest of 1 lemon (preferably unwaxed),
    grated
a pinch of freshly grated nutmeg

250ml (9fl oz) dry white wine
12 oysters (optional)
1 small shallot, peeled and finely
    chopped
1 tablespoon plain flour
stock or water, to taste
½ teaspoon salt

If the butcher has rolled and tied the meat, cut the string and unroll it to expose the inside. Scatter over the marjoram, lemon zest, a generous grating of nutmeg and the salt. Re-roll and tie firmly.

Preheat the oven to 220°C, 425°F, Gas mark 7. Put the meat into a roasting tin and cook for about 30 minutes. Baste with the wine, sprinkle the surface of the meat with salt, and reduce the heat to 180°C, 350°F, Gas mark 4. Continue to cook until done to your taste. Baste with the cooking juices at intervals.

When the meat is done, remove to a warmed serving plate and leave to rest. Pour all the roasting juices out of the tin into a bowl and allow the fat to rise; skim off as much as possible and reserve.

If using, open the oysters, strain their liquor through a sieve lined with kitchen paper to catch any bits of shell or sand, and reserve in a separate bowl.

Add about 2 tablespoons of the fat back to the roasting tin, heat gently and cook the chopped shallot in it until translucent. Add the flour and continue stirring and cooking until lightly browned. Stir in the roasting juices to make a smooth gravy. If using oysters, add their liquor at this point, stirring, and bring to a simmer. Just before serving, stir in the oysters and cook gently for a few minutes. They must be thoroughly hot. Otherwise, proceed as for a conventional gravy, adding a little stock and adjusting the seasoning to taste.

Lamb's Liver with Orange

Liver gained a bad reputation in British cookery, probably through school meals when it was served cooked to a texture like shoe leather. If stewed gently with plenty of seasonings until just cooked, it is very different.

serves 4

about 30g (1oz) fat – lard
    or beef dripping
1 large onion, peeled and
    thinly sliced
1 garlic clove, peeled and crushed
400g (14oz) lamb's liver, cut into
    thin slices

20g (¾oz) flour
zest of ½ orange, finely grated; and
    the juice of the whole orange
about 150ml (5fl oz) strong
    beef stock
a pinch of chilli powder
salt and black pepper

Melt the fat in a frying pan. Fry the onion and garlic gently until transparent, then remove them with a slotted spoon and put on one side. Dust the liver with flour and fry lightly on both sides. Stir any remaining flour into the fat, then add the onions and garlic back to the pan. Stir in the orange zest and juice, the stock, a small pinch of chilli powder, 1 scant teaspoon salt and a generous grind of black pepper. Stir well, then cover and cook on a low heat.

Test after 5 minutes by inserting the end of a sharp knife into one of the liver slices – if the juices run very red, cook for another 5–10 minutes. It's nicest if the meat is just cooked. Taste and add more seasoning if desired.

Serve immediately with a bowl of fluffy mashed potato.

Pork, Ham and Gammon

PORK COMES FROM PORKERS. This may seem a statement of the obvious, but pigs are graded by age and weight. A porker is a relatively young pig, which has achieved the optimum weight for fresh meat but is not large enough for salting for bacon and ham. Pigs for fresh pork can be grown on to be older and heavier, but the economics of feed versus the return on the meat come into play. In some cultures, pork is taboo but in the past, to the poor of the British Isles, and much of Europe, it often provided the small amount of meat they ate for most of the year.

Buying pork

Pork, like beef and lamb, has been bred for lean meat over the past 30–40 years as tastes have changed and people want less fat. Pork that is very lean is dull in flavour and dry in texture. On the other hand, no one wants to pay for large amounts of fat. To produce really good pork, as with other meat, a balance has to be struck. Tradition conflicts with the economics of bringing an animal to the optimum weight for meat in the shortest possible time with the highest proportion of lean and desirable prime meat. Pragmatism usually wins, and lean commercial stock is used for porkers, but this is not very flavoursome. Some butchers make a point of sourcing traditional and rare breed meat from slightly older animals, because the slower growth means more flavour. What the pig eats also makes a difference to flavour and the texture of the fat.

Another factor in the flavour of pork is something that is called 'boar taint'. While male cattle and some sheep destined for meat are castrated, in Britain, male pigs are left intact, and this can lead to a distinctive flavour in the meat – musky is probably the most polite way to describe it. The issues behind this relate both to animal welfare and the commercial implications to do with the way the animal gains weight. The theory is that taint will not be a problem since pigs are slaughtered for pork before puberty (the age at which boar taint develops, as a result of hormonal changes). However, other factors operate: some pigs have more of the flavour, or enter puberty at a younger than average age, while some people are more sensitive to the flavour. The only way to counter this problem is to know your supplier.

When you are buying pork, you should always look for lean meat that is pale pink, moist but firm; the fat should be white, firm but tender and present in reasonable but not excessive amounts. To store pork, remove the shop wrappings as soon as you get home, then cover it loosely and place on a clean plate or tray in the coolest part of the refrigerator.

Cuts for roasting and roasting times

Because the lean is tender and the fat usually ample, most cuts of pork are suitable for roasting. The loin and leg contain the highest proportion of lean meat in large muscles. A whole leg of pork is a big joint that tends to be dry if not carefully cooked. Forequarter cuts tend to be fattier and have more connective tissue, but they still roast well, especially slowly. If it's crackling that you want, choose a piece of loin, a joint fairly even in shape along its entire length; it can produce spectacular results. Loin, as with other animals, has a long tender undercut (often sold separately as fillet); if you are fortunate, it will be left in place, an extra treat.

Most people would consider removing the skin to be a waste, but if you want a less fatty result, or to marinate the meat, this is a necessity. The skin on all pork joints should be scored, to help it crisp, and to divide it after cooking – most butchers will do this for you.

Stuffing, including that old-fashioned mixture of sage and onion, is sometimes used for flavour as well as to counteract dryness in cuts such as leg. Other traditional flavourings for pork tend to fall into three categories: fruity, aromatic and sweet. In Britain, apple sauce or baked apples provide the former and are especially good with a really well-produced traditional-breed meat, the sweetness of the apple picking up on the inherent sweet note of well-fed pork. Lemon zest is also a good flavouring for pork, especially when paired with rosemary, thyme, fennel, garlic and black pepper. Chinese culture has provided a different range of flavourings, especially star anise, five-spice powder, and soy sauce in combinations with sugar or honey. These go particularly well with slow-roast pork and have become an important part of our modern culinary repertoire. Traditionally the British have not marinated pork, but if you are using aromatic herbs, sprinkle them over the meat and rub in some time before roasting (even the night before).

Do bear in mind that pork should always be thoroughly cooked. A rule of thumb for all cuts is to start the meat in a hot oven at 230°C, 450°F, Gas mark 8 for 20 minutes, then reduce the oven temperature to 170°C, 325°F, Gas mark 3 and allow 25 minutes per 500g for prime cuts (such as leg and loin) or 30 minutes per 500g for other cuts. I prefer to cook belly pork and forequarter cuts in a slow oven at 140°C, 275°F, Gas mark 1 for 60 minutes per 500g.

A meat thermometer is especially useful when you are cooking ham or gammon. Because these are cured meats, they remain pink even when they are fully cooked, and therefore it is less easy to tell when they are done.

Crackling

How to get crackling to crackle is, to some extent, a matter of knowing your oven and working out the optimum time and temperature. Slow roasting is a more reliable way of producing crackling than fast roasting because it gives the skin longer to crisp up and is less likely to scorch the edges of the joint. A method frequently recommended is to rub the skin with olive oil and salt before cooking.

Whatever method is used, three points help to provide good results. The first is that the meat must have a reasonable covering of fat: look for a layer just over 1cm (½in) thick, certainly not less. The next is that the skin should be properly scored; this needs to be done neatly in parallel lines at intervals of about 1cm (½in) apart, to about the same depth. The cuts might go down to the lean, but should not penetrate it. The third point is that the skin should be dry when the meat is put into the oven. This makes the following method seem rather strange, but it does work:

• Put the pork, skin-side up, on a rack in the sink. Boil a kettleful of water and immediately pour it evenly over the skin, allowing it to drain straight away. The skin will dry quickly as the residual hot water evaporates. Blot with kitchen paper or a clean cloth, then salt and roast as normal.

If the meat is cooked but the crackling has failed to crisp up, free it – as a sheet – from the meat and put it in a roasting tin. Cook at 200°C, 400°F, Gas mark 6, for 5–10 minutes. Cut it into strips.

Cooking pork in casseroles and stews

Pork casseroles are something of a rarity in English cookery, but pig meat still went into many stews. As lardons or as rashers wrapped round other meats, bacon gave fat and flavour to lean cuts of meat, poultry and game. It remains a vital ingredient in many dishes, giving an underlying, salty savouriness to stews in the grand tradition of ragoos and braises.

Ham was also used. Essence of ham was essential to fashionable kitchens in the 18th century: it was made by cutting a raw ham into slices, which were stewed with root vegetables, veal stock, mushrooms, truffles and spices. Eventually it was strained and the liquor kept for adding to other dishes. Hams were also braised. According to John Nott, in his *Cook's Dictionary* (1726), these were served hot with a ragoo of veal sweetbreads, chicken livers, cockscombs, mushrooms and truffles, or even sometimes crayfish.

Clearly, pork was valuable as a preserved meat: fine hams graced the tables of the rich; soused or collared pork was stored up by careful housewives; and innumerable barrels of salt pork were carried in the stores of sailing ships. Farmers and cottagers grew pigs on to bacon weight and salted as much as possible of the meat. Bacon goes much further than fresh pork to add savour to otherwise bland food, something well known to the less wealthy. Friedrich Engels, observing the lives of industrial workers in the 1840s in Manchester, noted how the poorest used small amounts of bacon to flavour the potatoes that were their staple food; a lack of this small resource was symptomatic of total destitution.

Probably because of its usefulness as preserved meat, fresh pork was unusual in stewed dishes in English cookery. Small cuts of pork, such as loin chops, seem to have been grilled for preference. Maybe pork stews simply fell through a social black hole – not smart enough to go into cookery books, too simple or commonplace to be noted elsewhere. That said, there is little evidence of poorer people stewing pork, except as faggots – a type of meatball made from pork meat and offal braised in stock, a dish of the rural tradition.

Cuts for casseroles, stews and pies
When cooking pork, a certain amount of fat distributed through the meat is desirable. Lean cuts such as leg or loin tend to be dry. Shoulder meat or spare rib chops (cut from the roasting joint, not the rack of ribs) are the best for stews. Belly pork, cut into large dice or used in one piece for braising is also a possibility, but remove the skin (which can be added to the braising liquid) and trim off any excess fat before cooking. A pig's trotter is also a good addition to many dishes.

Bacon for stews needs to be a traditionally produced dry-cured variety, not too lean. After all, what is required is fat and flavour, which is more concentrated in dry-cured meat. Pancetta can be used instead, and is often easier to buy as ready-cut lardons or in a thick slab that can be cut up as needed. Always use unsmoked meat unless otherwise stipulated. When choosing ham, fat is less desirable, but similar rules about dry curing and lack of smoke apply. A handful of bacon or ham lardons fried until crisp and then drained well enhance many stews; try them to garnish some of the fish recipes such as Haddock, Leek and Potato Stew with Mussels (see page 208) or Sarah's Summer Vegetable Stew (see page 212).

English fresh sausages are quite different from those of European countries, and the variety of those made by craft butchers has expanded way beyond the boundaries of English tradition in the past 20 years. It is well worth trying them out in a pulse-based casserole – for instance, with beans or lentils in a sauce (see page 124).

Flavourings and accompaniments
Apples and apple drinks are often used with pork. Cider is also sometimes cited as a cooking liquid: English ciders can be assertive in flavour, so go cautiously with them or mix with a little apple juice. White wine or verjuice make good substitutes. Pork shares, to some extent, the pale, mild qualities of veal and works well in some recipes that were originally intended for the latter. These are quite numerous in early cookery books.

Slow-Roast Belly Pork with Root Vegetables & Oriental Flavourings

serves 4

a piece of belly pork, weighing about
1.5kg (3½lb), with the skin scored
2–3 large baking potatoes
1 large carrot
1 sweet potato
2 large parsnips
2–3 small white turnips, or about
one-third of a larger yellow turnip
about 1 tablespoon oil or pork dripping
fresh root ginger, about 2cm (¾in),
peeled and cut into long matchsticks
a few shallots, peeled and halved
lengthways

6–8 garlic cloves, peeled but left whole
salt

For the oriental flavourings
2–3 whole star anise
generous 1 teaspoon whole black
peppercorns, lightly crushed
40g (1½oz) honey
2 tablespoons soy sauce
2 tablespoons dry sherry
200–300ml (7–10fl oz) chicken stock
(keep about a third of this back for
the end)

Preheat the oven to 220°C, 425°F, Gas mark 7. Give the pork the boiling water treatment (see page 69), and salt lightly. Mix all the oriental flavourings in a small bowl. Wash, trim and peel all root vegetables. Cut into chunks. Put them in a pan, cover with cold water and bring to the boil for about 2 minutes. Drain thoroughly. Heat the oil in a roasting tin until very hot, add the vegetables and turn them. Mix in the ginger, shallots and garlic. Pour over the flavourings and put the pork on top, skin side up.

Roast for 15 minutes, then reduce the heat to 150°C, 300°F, Gas mark 2. Cook for 2–3 hours; stir the vegetables once or twice.

About 30 minutes before you want to eat, turn the heat back up to 200°C, 400°F, Gas mark 6. Stir the vegetables, then return the tin to the oven. When the crackling is crisp, remove the meat to a warmed serving platter. Arrange the vegetables around it. Keep hot.

Skim the fat off the juices left in the roasting tin. Taste and add more salt if needed. Use hot stock to thin and deglaze any residue in the tin, then pour all juices, into a gravy boat.

a

Roast Loin of Pork with Sage and Onion Puddings

**serves
6**

a piece of pork loin, about 2.5kg
(5½lb)
150ml (5fl oz) dry white wine
generous 1 tablespoon plain flour
250ml (9fl oz) stock
(pork or chicken)
salt and pepper

For sage and onion puddings
pork or beef dripping for frying,
and for the pudding tins
1 small onion, peeled and chopped
half the quantities given for Yorkshire
Pudding (see page 25)
12 sage leaves, chopped

Preheat the oven to 230°C, 450°F, Gas mark 8. Prepare the pork for roasting in a tin. Calculate the roasting time. Roast for 20 minutes, then reduce the heat to 170°C, 325°F, Gas mark 3. After about 1 hour, add the white wine to the tin.

Meanwhile, prepare the sage and onion puddings. Melt the fat in a frying pan and cook the onion gently until translucent. Turn off the heat and allow to cool.

Cook the meat until done, checking from time to time. Remove from the oven and allowed to rest for at least 20 minutes before carving. Turn up the heat to 220°C, 425°F, Gas mark 7.

Make the Yorkshire pudding batter, then stir in the cooled onion and the chopped sage. Using a muffin tray or deep-holed bun tin, put 1 scant teaspoon of fat in each mould and then put into the oven to heat. When the fat is smoking hot, take the muffin tray out and add 1–2cm (½–¾in) to each mould. Return to the oven and cook for 15–20 minutes, or until puffed and golden, and done in the middle.

To make the gravy, pour all the juices out of the roasting tin into a bowl. Set aside for a few minutes then remove as much fat as possible to a separate container.

Put about 2 tablespoons of the fat back into the roasting tin and add the flour. Stir well over low heat, allowing the flour to brown. Stir in the defatted juices, scraping up any residue stuck to the tin. Gradually add the stock (you may not need it all), stirring well, and bring to the boil. Season to taste.

Pork with Garlic and Herb Paste

serves 4

a piece of belly pork, weighing about 2kg (4½lb)

1 tablespoon each of fresh sage, rosemary and mint, finely chopped

8 garlic cloves, peeled and crushed

grated zest of 1 lemon (preferably unwaxed)

a good pinch of finely ground allspice

a good pinch of finely ground coriander

1–2 tablespoons olive oil

a splash of white wine or stock

about 1 tablespoon plain flour

1 teaspoon salt

a generous grind of black pepper

Put the pork on a board and carefully cut through the fat layer between the skin and the meat (it helps if the pork is well chilled). Aim to leave just under 1cm (½in) fat attached to the skin, but don't worry too much if it is not possible. Keep the skin on one side and put the meat, bones down, in a roasting tin.

Mix all the ingredients except the white wine and flour to make a paste. Spread this evenly over the top of the meat. Put the skin back on top. Leave to marinate for 2–3 hours.

Preheat the oven to 140°C, 275°F, Gas mark 1 and put the pork in to cook. Allow at least 60 minutes per 500g, possibly a little longer. It will yield a lot of fat and some deep-brown juices.

When the meat is cooked, remove it to a warmed plate. If the crackling hasn't crisped, put it in a shallow tin, turn the oven up to 200°C, 400°F, Gas mark 6 and return it to cook for 10–15 minutes, checking progress occasionally. Pour off all the fat and juices from the roasting tin into a bowl. Deglaze the tin with white wine or stock and add to the juices. Skim off the fat.

Put 2 tablespoons of fat back into the roasting tin and add a little flour, stirring with a wooden spoon over a low heat. Allow the flour to cook and brown a little, then stir in the cooking juices, and a little more stock if necessary, to produce gravy.

To serve, cut the meat in slices. This is best served with cabbage and plainly cooked potatoes – mashed, or small whole new ones.

Loin of Pork Stuffed with Spinach

serves 4

1kg (2¼lb) boned pork loin
a little lemon zest (preferably
    unwaxed), finely grated
1 tablespoon olive oil
salt and pepper

For the spinach stuffing
250g (9oz) spinach, any thick stems
    removed
50g (2oz) parsley, stems removed
½ teaspoon salt
freshly ground black pepper

Choose a pork loin with a good proportion of lean meat. Remove the skin with the fat beneath, plus the 'tail' of fatty meat. The lean meat has a thin white covering of sinew over one side. Use a sharp knife to separate it from the lean.

Place the meat so that the grain is at right angles to you. Take a sharp knife and make a cut into the left side, parallel to the grain and about one-third of the way down from the top. Don't cut all the way through – leave a 'hinge' at the right-hand side. Now start at the right-hand side and repeat the action, cutting about one-third of the way up from the bottom, leaving the 'hinge' at the left.

Open out the meat as a single sheet like a leaflet. Sandwich it between 2 pieces of greaseproof paper and beat out with a rolling pin until it is roughly 1½–2 times larger, and about half the original thickness. Season with the lemon zest and salt and coarsely ground black pepper. Put to one side while you make the stuffing.

Wash the spinach and pack into a saucepan. Cook over high heat for a couple of minutes, stirring until it has wilted. Add the parsley and cook just enough to soften it. Remove from the heat, press into a sieve to get rid of the liquid. Put the mixture on to a board and chop coarsely. Season with the salt and pepper.

Take the meat and spread the spinach and parsley mixture over it, leaving about an inch all round. Roll up like a Swiss roll and tie firmly with string. Preheat the oven to 200°C, 400°F, Gas mark 6. Put the olive oil in a small roasting tin, then add the meat and roast for about 50 minutes. Check to make sure the outside isn't cooking too fast, and season the outside with salt about halfway through cooking. To carve, simply cut in thin slices.

Pork Marinated to Taste like Wild Boar

serves 6–8

2.5–3kg (5½–6½lb) leg of pork, boned and skinned
400ml (14fl oz) pork chicken or veal stock
3 tablespoons plain flour
salt and pepper

For the marinade
300ml (10fl oz) red wine
50ml (2fl oz) red wine vinegar
½ onion, peeled and sliced

2 shallots, peeled and sliced
2 garlic cloves, peeled and crushed
3 bay leaves, crushed
8–10 thyme sprigs
a few parsley stalks, roughly chopped
12 black peppercorns, bruised
12 juniper berries, bruised
3 cloves, bruised
zest of ½ orange (preferably unwaxed), cut in long strips
1 teaspoon salt

Put all the marinade ingredients in a saucepan and bring to the boil. Allow to cool.

Lightly score the fat of the meat in a diamond pattern. Put it in a deep bowl, and pour the cooled marinade over the meat. Turn it in the mixture, then cover and store in the refrigerator, where it can marinate for up to 4 days. Turn the meat a couple of times each day.

When ready to cook, preheat the oven to 220°C, 425°F, Gas mark 7. Remove the meat from the marinade. Strain the latter, reserving the liquid. Put the meat on a rack in a roasting tin and add a little water to the base of the tin. Cook for 20 minutes, then reduce the heat to 170°C, 325°F, Gas mark 3 for a further 2 hours, or until done. Baste with the reserved marinade at intervals and check that the liquid in the tin doesn't burn. If it becomes too deep brown, add a little more water to the tin – the gravy is very rich but will burn easily.

When the meat is cooked, remove to a warm serving dish and allow it to rest. Pour all the fat and juices from the tin into a bowl, then deglaze the tin with a little of the stock and add this to the juices. The fat will rise to the surface – skim off as much as possible. Put about 3 tablespoons of the fat back into the tin and sprinkle in the flour. Stir well and allow to cook gently over low heat. Once it has turned a creamy colour, gradually stir in the reserved cooking juices, then the stock. Taste and check the seasoning before serving.

Belly Pork Braised with Cider

Belly pork is usually cooked by roasting, but it is good rolled around a seasoning of herbs, braised gently and served cold – better than leaner cuts that tend to be dry. Choose the meat carefully, looking for a reasonable but not excessive layer of fat on top. Ask your butcher to remove the skin and bones, but take them home for the stock.

serves
6

about 1kg (2lb 4oz) piece of belly
    pork, skin and bones trimmed
    and reserved
generous pinch chilli powder
1 teaspoon fennel seeds, bruised
2 tablespoons finely chopped parsley
leaves from 6–8 sprigs thyme

2 garlic cloves, cut into slivers
zest of 1 lemon
15g (½oz) lard
200ml (7fl oz) cider
200ml (7fl oz) stock (preferably
    beef)
salt and black pepper

Put the pork, fat side down, on a board. Sprinkle with salt and grind a generous quantity of black pepper over it. Scatter with the chilli powder, fennel seeds, parsley, thyme, garlic and lemon zest. Roll up and tie firmly. The pork can be left overnight if desired.

When ready to cook, heat the lard in a flameproof casserole that will hold the meat neatly. Brown on all sides, then pour in the cider and let it bubble. Add the stock and bring to a gentle simmer. Tuck the skin and bones down beside the meat. Cover and transfer to a moderate oven, 160°C, 325°F, Gas mark 3, for 2½–3 hours, by which time the pork should be very tender.

Remove from the cooking liquor and allow it to cool a little. Wrap in greaseproof paper, put between two boards and press lightly – a 900g (2lb) weight or a couple of cans of tomatoes on top is adequate. Leave until cold. Taste the cooking liquor and season if necessary. Strain into a bowl and chill, then remove any fat from the top. The stock should set to a jelly.

To serve, cut the pork into very thin slices. Chop the jelly and use it as a garnish. Serve with a salad of mixed leaves tossed in a mustardy dressing.

Pork with Apple Juice and Quinces

Pork and apples go well together, whether it's because the pigs have been feeding on windfalls in an orchard or the meat has been cooked with apples or their products. This recipe uses apple juice but replaces the more usual sliced apples in the sauce with quinces – a related species, but with a distinctive perfumed aroma. Use a potato peeler to peel off the lemon zest.

serves 4

30g (1oz) butter
4 pork spare rib steaks, total weight
   about 800g (1lb 12oz)
2cm (¾in) length of cinnamon stick,
   ground
8 cloves, ground
1 teaspoon peppercorns, ground
a thumb-sized piece of fresh root
   ginger, peeled and cut into thin
   matchsticks

3–4 strips lemon zest
350ml (12fl oz) apple juice
1 dessertspoon soft brown sugar
1 large or 2 small quinces, cut into
   quarters, the pips and core removed
about 1 teaspoon salt

Melt the butter in a flameproof casserole and brown the pork on both sides. Remove it and keep to one side. Add the ground spices, the ginger and the strips of lemon zest to the residual butter and cook gently, stirring all the time, for 3–4 minutes. Then pour in the apple juice, bring to the boil and cook until the liquid has reduced by about a third.

Stir in the brown sugar, and add the pork, quinces and salt. Seal, covering the dish with foil and the lid, if it has one. Put in the oven at 140°C, 275°F, Gas mark 1, and cook for about 2 hours, or until the pork is tender.

Serve with a mixture of potatoes and parsnips mashed together.

Pork Meatballs with Saffron Sauce

This recipe was inspired by a dish of small pear-shaped meatballs, which appears in several cookery books of the late 17th and early 18th centuries. The original was based on veal, but the recipe works well with pork. The egg yolk and lemon juice thickening gives the sauce a pleasing acid note, good with the rich meat.

serves
4

400g (14oz) minced pork
50g (2oz) fresh white breadcrumbs
leaves from 3–4 sprigs thyme
1 generous tablespoon finely
 chopped parsley
zest of 1 lemon, and the juice
 of ½ lemon

about ¼ teaspoon ground cloves
2 eggs, separated
pinch of saffron threads
300ml (10fl oz) stock, pork
 or chicken for preference
sage leaves and stems, to serve
salt and black pepper

Put the pork, breadcrumbs, thyme, parsley, lemon zest, cloves, 1 scant teaspoon salt and some pepper in a large bowl. Add the egg whites. Mix well and divide into 16 portions. For an authentically 17th-century look, roll into pear shapes, wider at one end than the other.

Heat a deep frying pan or a flameproof casserole. Add the saffron strands and let them toast gently for a moment – only enough to release their fragrance; don't let them burn. Pour in the stock and bring to the boil. Add the meatballs and simmer gently, turning two or three times, for 30–45 minutes.

Just before serving, beat the egg yolks with the lemon juice. Remove the meatballs to a warm serving dish. Off the heat, pour the egg and lemon mixture into the sauce. Heat very gently, stirring all the time, until the sauce has thickened a little and is thoroughly hot. Taste, correct the seasoning and pour around the meatballs. Garnish each 'pear' with a sage leaf and stem.

Serve the meatballs in the sauce with some plain boiled rice.

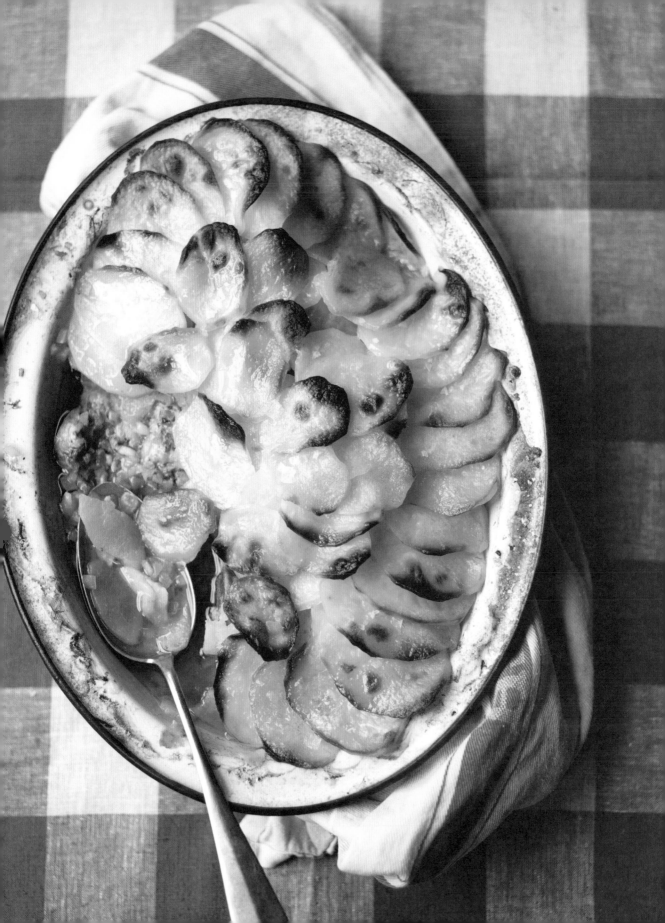

Pork with Potatoes and Apples

This is really a pork version of a hotpot. Verjuice is the juice of unripe grapes and it is available bottled from some delicatessens. It has a subtle sour-sweetness, which is good with all sorts of rich meat. If it is unavailable, then a mixture of white wine and lemon juice in the proportions of about 3:1 is the best substitute. Use a potato peeler to peel off the lemon zest.

serves 4

4 spare rib pork chops, total weight
    about 800g (1lb 12oz)
1 medium onion, peeled
2 garlic cloves, peeled
8 juniper berries
a strip of lemon zest

2 eating apples – Cox or russet for
    preference
120ml (4fl oz) verjuice
800g–1kg (1lb 12oz–2lb 4oz) potatoes
about 20g (¾oz) butter
salt

Put the meat in a deep ovenproof pie dish or casserole. Chop the onion, garlic, juniper berries and lemon zest together until quite fine. Mix with the pork, add salt, then cover and leave to marinate for 2 hours.

Peel and core the apples, then cut them into thin slices. Layer them over the pork. Pour in the verjuice. Then peel the potatoes and slice them thinly as well. Use them to cover the pork and apples, sprinkling lightly with salt and dotting with butter as you go. Cover the top with buttered greaseproof paper or foil and cook in a low oven, 140°C, 275°F, Gas mark 1, for 2 hours. At the end of this time, turn the heat up to 200°C, 400°F, Gas mark 6, remove the cover and allow the top layer of potatoes to brown and crisp.

Sausage and Lentil Stew

The fresh sausages of British tradition often lack the robustness and seasoning power of their European cousins, but are still good with lentils, echoing the long-time combination of pork with pulses. A well-made Cumberland sausage, which is meaty and highly peppered, is good for this recipe. If properly made, it should arrive coiled up in a long piece, rather than formed into links. Cut into suitable lengths before cooking.

serves
4

1 tablespoon lard, goose fat or olive oil
1 medium onion, chopped fairly finely
leaves from 3–4 sprigs rosemary,
   chopped
4 garlic cloves, peeled and chopped
600–700g (1lb 5oz–1lb 8oz)
   good-quality pork sausages

200ml (7fl oz) red wine
300g (11oz) small green lentils
   or Puy lentils
400ml (14fl oz) water
1 tablespoon Dijon mustard
salt and black pepper

Heat the fat or oil in a heavy frying pan or flameproof casserole. Add the onion, rosemary and garlic and cook briskly, turning frequently, until the onion begins to brown in patches. Add the sausages and allow to cook gently, turning every so often so that they brown a little.

Pour in the wine and let it bubble, then add the lentils, water and a good grinding of black pepper. Bring to the boil, transfer to a casserole, cover and put into the oven at 160°C, 325°F, Gas mark 3.

Cook for about 30 minutes, then check progress. If the lentils seem to be drying out, add a little more water, preferably boiling. Return to the oven for another 20–30 minutes, after which the lentils should be soft but still holding their shape. Stir in the mustard and then taste and check the seasoning – the sausages will probably have made the mixture salty enough, but add a little more as necessary.

Serve with a salad of watercress or other sharp leaves, and some good bread.

Faggots

Faggots are little bundles of pork meat and offal, wrapped in caul fat (a transparent membrane laced with fat, which lines the abdominal cavity of pigs and other meat animals). They belong to the now-extinct rural tradition of pig killing, and in the first half of the 20th century became the food only of the poor. Recipes for them underwent a certain amount of innovation, when the idea of the gastropub first evolved in the late 1990s. This is my own updated version.

serves 4–6

200g (7oz) boneless pork such as loin steaks – try to buy some with a reasonable amount of fat, about 25% of the total
200g (7oz) pork liver
200g (7oz) stewing veal
100g (3½oz) bacon, rinds removed
1 generous tablespoon chopped parsley
1 generous teaspoon chopped marjoram
1 generous teaspoon thyme leaves (lemon thyme if possible)

2 large garlic cloves, peeled and crushed
100g (3½oz) shallots, peeled and finely chopped
1 teaspoon salt
2 tablespoons brandy
zest of 1 lemon, finely grated
a piece of caul fat from a pig
300ml (10fl oz) strong stock from pork, chicken or beef
black pepper

Mince the pork, liver, veal and bacon together and put in a bowl. Add all other ingredients except the caul fat and stock. Season with pepper. Mix with your hands to make sure everything is evenly distributed. Divide the mixture into 18–20 equal pieces and form into balls.

Put the caul fat into a bowl of tepid water for a few minutes. Carefully unravel it to give a large sheet. Use kitchen scissors to cut it into small pieces, about 8cm (3¼in) square, avoiding any bits that are very fatty. Drain the pieces and wrap each ball of faggot mixture in one, trimming any excess caul.

Put the faggots in a baking dish that holds them neatly. Pour the stock around them, and bake in a moderate oven, 180°C, 350°F, Gas mark 4, for about 1 hour. They should be cooked through and the tops nicely browned. At the end of cooking time, pour off the cooking juices (keep the faggots warm in a low oven), allow the fat to rise and skim off as much as possible. Then reheat to boiling, pour back around the faggots and serve.

Normandy Pork Stew

This is a variation on an original recipe for harrico of mutton, given by Eliza Acton (1845). Pork loin chops work well with the new potatoes in this recipe.

serves
4

500–600g (1lb 2oz–1lb 5oz) pork chops from the loin or spare rib
1 tablespoon flour
20g (¾oz) butter or oil such as sunflower
300–400ml (10–14fl oz) light pork or chicken stock
4 spring onions, washed, trimmed and tied in a bunch with some parsley stems

500–600g (1lb 2oz–1lb 5oz) small new potatoes, scrubbed or scraped as preferred
salt and black pepper
chopped parsley, to garnish

Trim the chops of any excess fat. Mix the flour, 1 teaspoon salt and some pepper, and dust the chops with it. Heat the butter or oil in a large frying pan and brown the chops on both sides.

Sprinkle in any leftover flour and stir to amalgamate with the fat. Stir in the stock and bring to the boil. Add the spring onions and the parsley stems. Cover, reduce the heat and allow the stew to simmer very gently for 30–45 minutes. At the end of this time, add the potatoes in a single layer on top of the meat. Cover and continue to cook for about 30 minutes, or until the potatoes are tender.

Remove from the heat, fish out the parsley and spring onions and discard them. Allow to settle for a few minutes, then skim off any excess fat. Check the seasoning and adjust if necessary. Scatter a little chopped parsley over each portion.

Roast Ham or Gammon

When cooking ham, boiling is often thought of as the standard method, but opinions have always been split over this, and both spit-roasting and baking were also used. There are two basic ways to finish a ham, either by glazing or by dredging with breadcrumbs (see opposite), recalling the 17th- and 18th-century spit-roasts.

serves
8

a piece of uncooked ham or gammon,
    without skin, weighing 2kg (4½lb)
a handful of cloves (optional)
a glaze or breadcrumb coating
    (see opposite)

Follow the supplier's instructions about whether or not to soak the ham and for how long. If the piece of meat is to be served glazed, score the fat in diamonds at about 2cm (¾in) intervals and stud with cloves.

Preheat the oven to 170°C, 325°F, Gas mark 3, then put the meat in a roasting tin and cover with a sheet of foil. Bake for 30 minutes per 500g, and 30 minutes extra. For the last 30 minutes, remove the foil to allow the outside of the joint to brown, or use one of the finishes opposite.

Glaze for Ham

125ml (4fl oz) whisky, preferably
   without smoky character
125g (4½oz) demerara sugar

zest of ½ orange (preferably unwaxed),
   cut in very thin strips
1 piece of star anise (optional)

Mix together all the ingredients, without dissolving the sugar. About 30 minutes before the end of cooking time, remove any covering from the meat and pour this mixture over it. If some of the sugar crystals remain on top, so much the better, because they will crisp a little during cooking. Use the mixture that runs into the tin and combines with the cooking juices to baste the meat at frequent intervals during the remaining cooking time.

Breadcrumb Coating

4 tablespoons breadcrumbs made from
   stale white bread
1 tablespoon very finely chopped parsley

The breadcrumbs are best made by putting a couple of slices of stale white bread in a low oven. Leave them until they are dried out and pale gold, then remove, cool and crush. The crumbs need to be quite fine: pulverise the bread in a food processor or beat it in a mortar to reduce it as much as possible. Then rub through a wire sieve. Most will pass through to become near-powder. A few will remain in the sieve, but the process should reduce these to a degree of fineness that is acceptable, so use these too and mix in the parsley.

Put the mixture on a sheet of greaseproof paper. About 30 minutes before the end of cooking time, remove the foil from the meat and roll the side with the fat on over the crumb mixture, using the paper to help pat it over the surface. Return to the oven and cook for a further 30 minutes or until the coating is golden brown.

Roast Ham with Rhenish Wine

'Rhenish' wine (from the Rhineland vineyards) was much appreciated in Britain during the 17th and 18th centuries. Whether it had the same perfumed notes and degree of sweetness that it does today is not clear, but this recipe, after one given by John Thacker in 1758, is worth trying.

serves 6–8

a piece of unsmoked ham weighing about 2–2.5kg (4½–5½lb)
a handful of cloves (optional)
1 bottle light, medium-sweet German wine, such as Niersteiner

scant 2 tablespoons plain flour
200ml (7fl oz) light stock
salt and pepper

Follow the supplier's instructions about whether or not to soak the ham.

When ready to cook, carefully remove the skin from the ham (try to leave most of the fat in place). If desired, score the fat and stud with cloves. Place the meat on a rack in a roasting tin and pour the wine in underneath.

Preheat the oven to 220°C, 425°F, Gas mark 7. Roast the meat for 30 minutes, then reduce the heat to 170°C, 325°F, Gas mark 3. Continue to cook, basting at frequent intervals with the wine. If this shows signs of drying up and catching, add a little water.

When the ham is done, remove to a warm serving plate to rest. Pour all the roasting juices into a bowl, allow the fat to rise and skim off as much as possible. Put about 2 tablespoons of the fat back in to the roasting tin and sprinkle in a little flour. Stir well, and allow to cook gently for a few minutes. Then gradually stir in the juices, scraping well with a wooden spoon to incorporate any residue from the base and sides of the roasting tin. Bring to the boil and stir in some stock to make a lightly thickened gravy. Check for seasoning: it is unlikely that much, if any, salt will be needed, but some grpound black pepper is a good addition. Also, if the meat has been cooked plainly, a couple of cloves crushed to powder can be added at this stage, to give just a hint of spice.

Serve with roast or mashed potatoes and greens.

Potted Ham

A good method for using up cold ham. Potting started off with raw meat cooked specifically for the purpose (it was actually a means of preserving, on a similar principle to French *confit d'oie*). Over the years, the recipes changed and became lighter and softer (and eventually evolved into the various 'pastes' sold as sandwich fillings).

serves
4

250g (9oz) cold cooked ham
freshly ground black pepper
ground mace, allspice or star anise
125g (4½oz) unsalted butter, softened

Take a piece of cold ham and remove any gristly bits, skin and connective tissue, and any outside edges that have hardened and browned in cooking (these can all go in the stockpot). Fat (unless there is an excessive amount, which is unlikely these days) can be incorporated into the potting process. Cut the ham into small chunks and then blitz it in a food processor. Add some black pepper and your other chosen seasonings. Mace and allspice are traditional; star anise isn't, but a suspicion, finely pounded, is good. Don't overdo the seasoning, and if you choose to add star anise, don't mix it with any other spices but pepper, and add a very small pinch – otherwise, it will be overpowering.

Beat the softened butter until creamy and mix in the seasoned ham. Put the mixture into a serving dish, such as a china soufflé dish, then chill. Serve for lunch or tea, with hot toast or good bread.

Chicken and Poultry

CHICKEN, TURKEY, GOOSE, GUINEA FOWL AND DUCK are all classified as poultry – domestic birds reared for the table. They were often seasonal, and were sought after as delicacies at particular times of the year, but as domestic birds they had less status than game, and were more accessible to the general population. We buy chickens all year round, expecting them to be tender and varying in price according to weight, along with other factors relating to the way in which they are produced. Our ancestors priced chickens differently – by age and time of year. In 1845, Eliza Acton wrote:

> Fowls are always in season when they can be procured sufficiently young to be tender. About February they become dear and scarce; and small spring chickens are generally very expensive. As summer advances they decline in price.

This relates directly back to the cycle of egg-laying and hatching, which was at its lowest point in mid-winter, but increased dramatically as soon as the days began to lengthen. The majority of birds hatched around Easter flooded the market and the price came down as summer went on. They grew much more slowly than modern commercial stock – whose swift growth rate would have seemed extraordinary to farmers in the past.

A spring chicken really was a spring chicken – hatched in mid- to late winter, and ready for the table as a luxury in spring. It was simply roasted and appreciated for its tender flesh and delicate flavour. Smaller birds, the equivalent of poussins, were available, and were often grilled; older fowls were also plentiful, but were more suitable for boiling. Capons (castrated cockerels) were also once much esteemed, as they grew to be large, fat table birds. Generally, we favoured young tender chickens – and that is what we now get, but at the price of compromising production systems, with repercussions for the welfare of the live birds, and a loss of flavour. It is difficult now to imagine what a luxury a roast chicken was right up until the 1960s.

Domestic chickens have come a very long way from their probable origin as wild south-east Asian jungle fowl that were slowly domesticated and gradually spread westwards, arriving in the British Isles shortly before the Roman conquest. From then they scratched around farmyards, dunghills and urban backyards, probably with little change over the centuries – until, like all other farm animals, they began to receive the attention of agricultural improvers in the 18th and 19th centuries. They were improved by an input from Asian strains, which caused quite a stir because of their decorative appearance. The process by which the changes happened is largely unrecorded, because poultry breeding was generally a hobby for the urban working class, especially in the north of England.

That said, many ladies – including Queen Victoria herself – kept fancy poultry as ornamental birds.

The counties around London, especially Surrey, Kent and Sussex, specialised in producing fat chickens for the London market, which showed a preference for white-fleshed birds. In the late 19th century, the creatures were crammed with oatmeal to give a fine flavour and texture. The ideal fowl was required to have lots of tender white breast meat and light bones; economics, as always, looked for a bird that was early maturing. 'Sussex' breeds of hen evolved from this demand, and the characteristics can still be detected in birds reared for the broiler system developed in the 1950s. The commercial breed used currently is the Ross Cobb, bred to gain weight as fast as possible and provide large amounts of white meat. In free-range systems with good feed it can produce a fine chicken, but doesn't show its best side when subjected to intensive broiler production.

At tables in the past, a plain roast chicken with bread sauce and stuffing was considered ideal for a Sunday dinner, and in the 18th century was served as a delicacy as part of a meal of multiple dishes. The traditional accompaniment of bread sauce dates back to the Middle Ages, when breadcrumbs were used to thicken and bind spiced sauces, although it was often badly made, with a texture described by Colonel Kenney-Herbert as being 'like a bread poultice'. The use of other flavours and sauces with chicken followed the general trends over the centuries, but the British developed dishes using large amounts of pungent aromatics such as tarragon or garlic under French influence.

Chicken has many other advantages. Roast chicken is excellent cold, and was a good dish for a ball supper (especially with mayonnaise and salad), or for a picnic. The meat could be made into other dishes, and the bones produce good stock – so they were sought after.

Guinea fowl, turkey, goose and duck

None of these birds are related in any way to chickens, but they are farmed for their meat in Britain. Guinea fowl and turkey have white flesh and flavours that are in the same range as chicken. Wild duck and guinea fowl are sometimes classed with game – guinea fowl because it is gamier than chicken and shares the same tendencies as pheasant to dryness.

Guinea fowl are indigenous to Africa; known in parts of the Mediterranean by Classical times, they became more widespread in early modern times through links between Guinea and Portugal (hence the English name). The live birds have attractive spotted plumage and a rounded, bustling shape. They have been used in British cookery since the 16th century or before, but there are few specific recipes for them, and they were often treated like turkey.

When turkeys arrived in Britain, shortly after European explorers discovered the Americas, they were an exotic curiosity. As a large bird, they were served at great feasts and on important occasions.

The association with Christmas developed early but not exclusively until the 19th century. Stuffings and forcemeats have always been used with turkey, especially pork sausagemeat and chestnuts.

European domestic ducks are probably descended from mallards, the typical wild ducks of the British countryside. Like geese, domestic ducks were often crossed by smallholders, the birds congregating around farm or village ponds. Domestic geese are probably descended from wild geese native to Europe, and for many centuries they were Christmas food. Because they need space and grass to graze on, they are resistant to intensive farming and remain highly seasonal.

Buying, storing and preparing chickens

As a child, I was privileged to live on a farm with ample opportunity to observe some (very) free-range hens. My favourite source now is a local farm shop run by a woman who takes enormous pride in her poultry flock, and an equal pride in their presentation — plump, properly plucked, nicely trussed, complete with giblets. The flavour is excellent. If you are buying chicken in a supermarket, always look at the quality symbols and aim for one that ensures the optimum in terms of space, access to outdoors and feed quality. The ability to range freely and a diet rich in grain will both make a considerable difference to the flavour of the bird.

Quality labels can help in making a choice. French Label Rouge birds should have been reared under excellent conditions with the best flavour in mind. They will be expensive. Supermarkets often have their own premium ranges, which make claims about welfare and feed. Individual producers (who mostly sell via their own shops and networks, or over the internet) often give a lot of detail about the conditions under which their birds are reared. Transparency in labelling, and in both supplier and producer, are all-important with chicken and poultry in general. The more anonymous a product, the less likely it is to have been treated with care at any stage.

When buying chicken, a poussin is a very small young bird, weighing 450–500g (1lb–1lb 2oz), which will feed one person. A chicken — an older bird, though perhaps no more than 6–8 weeks old – will weigh around 1.5kg (3½lb) and feed 4 people. Older, larger birds — up to about 2.5kg (5½lb), and sometimes bigger — will feed up to 6 people.

The less a chicken costs, the more likely it is to need attention when it arrives in the kitchen. As soon as you get home, remove and discard all the wrappings and elastic bands that have been used to truss the bird (if it is trussed with string stitched through from side to side, the chances are that it has been properly prepared, and you won't need to do much). Pluck out any stubs and bits of feather. Dry the skin with kitchen paper, and dry the inside of the bird as well. Remove any obvious bits of pipe and trim the skin of the neck neatly.

Chickens, and most other birds, used to arrive with a little package of giblets tucked neatly inside them — the neck, heart, gizzard and liver. You can use these, if there are any, to make good stock (see the recipe opposite). Very few chickens seem to come with giblets now. From the cook's point of view, this is not a good development.

The purpose of trussing a chicken is to make it look neat, compact and well shaped; to keep it tidy without any projecting bits to scorch (especially important for spit-roasting), ultimately giving a plump-looking bird which would present well at table. In practice, when roasting birds in the oven, I find that a trussed one tends to be undercooked between the thigh and the body when the rest of the bird is done. For this reason, I tend to remove ties about two-thirds of the way through cooking.

Buying, storing and preparing guinea fowl, turkey, goose and duck

Guinea fowl meat is similar to that of a good free-range chicken but it is both leaner and gamier in flavour. The birds are also smaller than chickens, and they generally weigh 1–1.5kg (2¼lb–3½lb). One bird will serve 3–4 people. Like chicken, it suffers from intensive rearing and as it is difficult to know what system has been used, generally you should assume this will have been intensive, unless it is stated otherwise.

Even a small turkey weighs 4–5kg (8½–11lb) and will feed 8 people, whereas monster birds of 8–10kg (17½–22lb) are not unusual. Most commercial turkeys are white-feathered, but if you want a bird with more flavour and slightly less breast meat, try to find a Norfolk black or a Kelly Bronze. Both are now available to order onlione. Remove the turkey from its packaging and blot it well inside and out with kitchen paper. Pick it over for stray feathers and store, covered, in the fridge. Remove it 1–2 hours before roasting. If using stuffing, prepare and cool it before filling the turkey to avoid the potential for food poisoning.

It's difficult to buy a welfare-friendly duck due to intensive farming methods. Duck has only a shallow layer of meat over the breastbone and yields a lot of fat, but it has a delicious flavour and a skin that can be roasted to a crisp texture. Even a relatively large duck will only serve 4 people. If you want really crisp skin, start the day before and part the skin from the fat layer below by pulling and pinching it with your fingers until it loosens. Put the duck on its front in a rack in the sink and pour a kettleful of boiling water over it. Turn it onto its back and repeat. Dry the skin and inside the bird thoroughly with kitchen paper. Put it on a rack in the bottom of the refrigerator to dry the skin until it feels like parchment.

A small goose weighs about 5kg (11lb) whereas a large one is about 7kg (15lb). Despite their size, they usually don't serve more than 6–8 people, with little in the way of leftover meat. The meat is deeper in flavour and richer than turkey, so portions can be smaller. Remove any wrappings as soon as possible and the pick the goose over for stray feathers. Wash the giblets thoroughly.

Chicken Giblet Stock

Should you manage to acquire a chicken with giblets, check the liver carefully to make sure the dark green gall bladder has been discarded. Add the liver to a stuffing mixture, pâté or a ragù for pasta.

Put the remaining giblets in a small pan with a bay leaf, a few parsley stalks and a few pieces of onion, carrot and celery if available, cover with water and bring to the boil. Skim, then cover and leave to simmer gently for about an hour. Top up with more water if necessary. Strain, discarding the debris and reserve the stock for gravy.

Roasting times

Chicken must always be well cooked. Underdone, it is a notorious source of food poisoning. Because of this, it is also better not to stuff the body cavity of the bird, as the heat may not reach the centre of the stuffing by the time the meat is done. Cook the stuffing in a separate dish. Occasionally a thin layer of stuffing or some kind of flavouring is spread between the skin and the meat of the breast, a method which adds flavour and fat to the meat underneath. Chicken, like turkey, is sometimes served with little sausages and bacon as well as bread sauce, or barded with bacon like game birds. If you don't bard it, protect the breast with buttered paper or foil during the early stages of cooking.

Standard instructions for roasting a chicken are to start it off at 200°C, 400°F, Gas mark 6 for 20 minutes, then reduce the heat to 180°C, 350°F, Gas mark 4 and cook for 20–25 minutes per 500g until the juices run clear. Examine the meat between the leg and the body; if any hint of pink shows here, or in the juices which flow from the thickest part of the thigh when pierced with a skewer, the bird needs further cooking. Starting the bird on its side, then turning on to the other side, and finally on to its back during cooking helps to get it cooked evenly. Always allow a little time for resting at the end of the cooking time.

Large turkeys are heavy and difficult to handle when they are hot, so make sure that you have a large enough roasting tin and also that the turkey is not too big to fit into your oven. It must be properly cooked. The meat has a tendency to dryness which long cooking exacerbates. The methods usually suggested for counteracting this include marinating, barding, basting and slow, gentle cooking. Marinating the bird overnight in some flavoured brine can help retain moisture. Bard the turkey with fat bacon, a butter-soaked cloth, or simply smear some softened butter over the breast of the bird. Basting by pouring the cooking juices and fat back over the turkey fairly frequently is always a good idea. Also effective is to start cooking with it lying on its side and then turning it, before finally turning it onto its back to complete the cooking.

Temperatures and times recommended for cooking turkey vary enormously, and they depend to some extent on the size of the bird. As a guideline, you should use 170°C, 325°F, Gas mark 3 for 30 minutes per 500g, but, as ever, be guided by personal experience, the quirks of individual ovens and your instinct at the time. When the bird is fully cooked, leave it to rest, covered, in a warm place. To carve, take slices of breast from front to back. Carve any stuffing or forcemeat in the crop across in slices. Take off the legs and wings (with a narrow outer portion of breast attached), and divide, carving slices off the thighs and drumsticks.

When roasting guinea fowl, start the bird on its side for 10 minutes, then turn it on the other side for another 10 minutes. Cook at 200°C, 400°F, Gas mark 6 and after 20 minutes reduce the heat to 180°C, 350°F, Gas mark 4. Continue cooking for about 25 minutes until done.

Duck needs a particularly strong heat to start it, so give it 20 minutes at 230°C, 450°F, Gas mark 8 before reducing the heat to 180°C, 350°F, Gas mark 4 and cooking for another 1–1½ hours, depending on size. Some people recommend cooking it for much longer, which helps to produce crisp skin but may dry out the meat. Use strong poultry shears to cut the bird into quarters when cooked. Stuffing is a matter of taste; sage and onion was favoured in the past but use this only if you intend to make a plain gravy. Duck is so rich and flavoursome that it is sometimes better served plain without a stuffing but with a sauce or marmalade. Oranges complement it perfectly.

Cooking poultry in stews, casseroles and pies

For the best flavour, buy the best and most carefully reared birds you can find. This goes for all poultry, but is especially true for chickens. It can't be said too often that they will taste better, their meat will have a firmer texture and their bones will make better stock.

Using chicken in stews

It is unusual now to braise or stew a chicken or other bird whole, although there is no reason why it shouldn't be done. But a chicken cut into joints or taken off the bone cooks more evenly, it is easier to serve and eat, and portions are easy to buy. Chicken for stewing or for pies generally looks neater if skinned; add the skin to the stockpot. Unless featuring a mature boiling fowl (a possibility now that keeping hens has become a popular hobby once more), a chicken stew cooks relatively fast. You should allow 1–1¼ hours for a small bird, but do check carefully to make sure the meat is adequately cooked. A whole bird might take a little longer, especially if it's large, and an older fowl should be allowed a good 2 hours at a slow simmer.

   The light fresh flavours of spring and summer vegetables and herbs always go well with the meat (see Fricassée of Chicken and Asparagus). Slightly acidic flavours, such as those of dry white wine and lemon juice, also work well with poultry, especially chicken, or you can try richer creamy sauces as in Turkey Fricassée, or wild mushrooms as a delicious accompaniment.

Using turkey in stews

Making stews with turkey is easier than it used to be. Formerly, one would have to buy the entire bird and cut it up, but turkey portions and diced turkey have taken the trouble out of this. Like chicken, it is important that the meat is fully cooked; also, meat from turkey legs needs time – allow about 1½ hours gentle stewing to make it tender. Apart from the recipes given in the following pages, turkey can be used in recipes for chicken; or try turkey escalopes cut from the breast as an alternative to veal in Veal Olives or in Veal and Ham Pie; and turkey mince instead of pork in Pork Meatballs with Saffron Sauce (see page 120), adding a light spicing of cayenne or chilli pepper – don't overdo it; a generous pinch is enough.

Using duck in stews

Duck, a much darker, denser and fattier meat, is delicious cooked gently in rich casseroles and stews. I've added flavours taken from East Asian cookery to update the 18th-century notions of Stewed Duck with Green Peas. Like other poultry, duck is now widely available in good supermarkets as well as butchers' shops in quarters or joints. If you don't want to cook the whole bird, use the legs, and leave the duck breasts for grills or other quickly cooked dishes.

Basic Roast Chicken

serves
4–5

½ lemon
1 chicken, weighing 2kg (4½lb)
a few sprigs of fresh herbs, such as
   parsley, thyme or marjoram
2 unsmoked bacon rashers (optional)
unsalted butter

3–4 tablespoons white wine or water
stock from the giblets or other chicken
   stock
scant 1 tablespoon plain flour
freshly ground black pepper
½ teaspoon salt

Preheat the oven to 200°C, 400°F, Gas mark 6. Put the lemon in the body cavity of the bird, along with the herbs. Bard the breast with bacon or spread a little butter on it. Spread a little butter over the roasting tin (just enough to stop the bird sticking as it starts to cook), and put the bird in. Calculate the roasting time.

Start roasting a chicken on its side. Cover with a lid or oiled or buttered foil. Roast for 20 minutes, then reduce the heat to 180°C, 350°F, Gas mark 4. After another 10 minutes, turn the bird on to the other side; cover and roast for 15–20 minutes. Turn it on to its back, add the wine or water, cover, and roast for 30 minutes.

Remove the foil, baste with the cooking juices and sprinkle the salt over the skin. Return, uncovered, to the oven for the remainder of the roasting time. Check every 10 minutes or so to make sure the juices aren't burning. If they show signs of overcooking, add a little water. The skin should crisp and brown nicely. Baste once or twice more with the cooking juices to produce a really crisp, tasty skin. The bird is done when the juices from the thickest part of the leg run clear (pierce it with a clean skewer or the tip of a sharp knife). Make sure the meat around the hip joint between the leg and the body is fully done; there should be no trace of pink. If there is, return the bird to the oven for a few minutes.

When cooked, remove from the roasting tin to a warm serving plate while you make the gravy. Pour all the juices into a bowl, deglaze the tin with a little stock and add the result to the rest of the juices. Return the tin to the heat, then add a couple of tablespoons of the fat that rises to the top of the cooking juices and stir in the flour, allowing it to cook gently and turn a nutty brown. Remove as much fat as possible from the remaining juice and then stir gradually into the mixture in the roasting tin. Stir in the giblet stock, taste and adjust the seasoning.

Chicken and Tomato Stew

A recipe derived from a stew my mother sometimes made. She used it for the hens from her poultry flock which had passed their prime, becoming what she called 'boiling fowl'. They were not as tender as chickens, but had lots of flavour.

serves 4–6

50g (2oz) butter or 4–5 tablespoons sunflower oil
1 large onion, finely chopped
2–3 garlic cloves, crushed
leaves from 1 sprig rosemary, chopped
30g (1oz) flour

1 large chicken, preferably free-range, about 2kg (4lb 8oz), skinned and jointed into 10–12 pieces
250ml (9fl oz) white wine
6–8 plum tomatoes, or 400g (14oz) canned tomatoes
salt and black pepper

Heat the butter or oil in a large frying pan. Add the onion, garlic and rosemary and fry briskly, stirring frequently, until the onion begins to form pale golden patches. Use a slotted spoon to transfer it to a casserole.

Season the flour and use to dredge the chicken pieces, then fry gently until golden in the fat used for frying the onion. Add the chicken pieces to the casserole.

Sprinkle any remaining flour into the pan and stir well, then pour in the white wine and keep stirring, scraping any up residues from the base of the pan. When the mixture has come to the boil, add it to the casserole.

If using fresh tomatoes, put them in a bowl, cover with boiling water for a couple of minutes, then drain them and peel off the skins. Cut each one in half, and add to the casserole. Canned tomatoes can be added as they are, straight from the tin, including the juice.

Cover and cook at 180°C, 350°F, Gas mark 4 for about 1½ hours. Taste and correct the seasoning. Serve with steamed or mashed potatoes, or rice.

Roast Chicken with Orange and Lemon

Citrus fruits were favourite flavourings for all sorts of meat dishes by the late 16th century, when they were used in combination with sweet spices and dried fruit. This recipe uses orange and lemon only, producing a very intense, slightly sharp-flavoured gravy.

serves
4–5

1 chicken, weighing 2kg (4½lb)
juice and pared zest of 1 lemon
   (preferably unwaxed)
juice and pared zest of 1 orange
   (preferably unwaxed)

a few sprigs of fresh herbs, such
   as parsley, thyme or
   marjoram (optional)
splash of stock, to deglaze
salt and pepper

Start the chicken off as in the basic method (see page 138). When you turn the chicken on to its back, pour the fruit juices over. Cover again and return to the oven. About 30 minutes before the end of cooking time, uncover, baste, then salt the skin and add the zest, cut in thin strips, to the juices and return to the oven. Baste again a couple more times. Take special care to watch that the juices in the tin don't burn; add extra stock or water if necessary.

At the end of cooking time, the bird should have a deep gold-brown and very crisp skin. Turn the oven up to 220°C, 425°F, Gas mark 7 for a few minutes to get it really brown and crisp at the end, if necessary, but do watch for burning. There should be a relatively small amount of juice with a very concentrated flavour in the roasting tin. Pour off the juices and deglaze the tin with a little stock. Skim the fat off the juices and add the deglazed cooking residue, but don't attempt to make a thickened gravy – just give everyone a spoonful or two of the cooking juices with the meat.

Roast Chicken with Tarragon

The fresh, grassy, slightly aniseed note of tarragon is a classic partner for chicken in French cookery, with many variations on the theme, using poached or roast chicken, served hot or cold. Although recipes for the dish have appeared in several English cookery books over the last 100 years or so, it never seems to have become really popular, perhaps because French tarragon is not especially easy to grow in Britain (Russian tarragon, much more vigorous, lacks the flavour of the French variety). This is based on a recipe given by Elizabeth David in *Summer Cooking* (1965).

serves 4–5

a small bunch of fresh tarragon
60g (2½oz) unsalted butter
1 chicken, weighing 2kg (4½lb)
1 teaspoon grated lemon zest
   (preferably unwaxed), plus
   ½ the lemon

100ml (3½fl oz) white wine or
   chicken stock
generous 1 teaspoon plain flour
150ml (5fl oz) single cream
salt and pepper

Pick the leaves off the tarragon and chop them. Mix a generous tablespoonful of chopped leaves with most of the butter – leave about 15g (½oz) for finishing the sauce. Put the tarragon butter, and the ½ lemon, inside the bird. Roast as in the basic method given on page 138, basting from time to time with the cooking juices, turning it on to its back after 45 minutes, and seasoning with salt and pepper towards the end of cooking.

When the bird is cooked, remove it to a warmed plate and pour all the juices into a bowl. Deglaze the tin with the white wine, making sure it bubbles fiercely, or with a little chicken stock. Add all the herby, buttery juices back into the roasting tin. Add the lemon zest and the remaining butter worked together with the flour. Stir well, then add the cream and the rest of the chopped tarragon and heat until the sauce boils and thickens.

Roast Pullet with Gammon

The original for this recipe came from John Nott in *The Cook's and Confectioner's Dictionary* (1726). His recipes reflect the rich, meaty dishes popular among the aristocracy of the early 18th century. A pullet – a young laying hen – was an especially prodigal use of resources.

serves 4

100g (4oz) lean gammon (or unsmoked bacon, fat removed)
2 tablespoons finely chopped fresh herbs – a mixture of parsley, chives and basil

1 chicken, on the small side – about 1.5kg (3½lb)
olive oil or unsalted butter
splash of chicken stock, to deglaze
salt and pepper

Preheat the oven to 180°C, 350°F, Gas mark 4. Mince the gammon. In an 18th-century kitchen, some unfortunate maid or scullion would have had to do this on a board with two knives; for us, a food processor works very well. Mix the minced meat with the chopped herbs, then season; go easy on the salt, as the gammon will already be salty, but be fairly generous with the pepper.

Carefully ease the skin away from the flesh over the breast of the chicken. Divide the gammon and herb mixture in two and spread it over each side of the bird, between the meat of the breast and the skin. Pull the skin back and sew or skewer it at the neck so that the stuffing remains in place during cooking.

Spread a little olive oil or butter in a roasting tin and put the bird in. Cover the breast with a piece of tinfoil, as the skin cooks through quickly in this recipe. (Start the bird off breast down if this works better in your oven, but when you turn it on to its back, use a piece of tinfoil to protect the breast until cooking is nearly completed.) Calculate the cooking time (see page 136) and roast until the bird is three-quarters cooked. Then remove the foil, baste well, sprinkle the bird with salt and continue roasting until fully cooked.

Put the bird on a warmed platter to rest, removing any strings or skewers. Skim the fat off the cooking juices and deglaze the pan with a little stock. Check the seasoning and serve.

Chicken Curry

serves
4

1 chicken or chicken portions, about
    1.5–2kg (3lb 4oz–4lb 8oz)
3 small onions, peeled and sliced
    (add the onion skin and trimmings
    to the stock)
1 carrot, trimmed and peeled
1 celery stick
a few black peppercorns
2 garlic cloves, peeled
1 dessertspoon turmeric
1 dessertspoon coriander seed, ground
1 teaspoon cayenne pepper

1 teaspoon sugar
1 teaspoon salt
2cm (¾in) cube of fresh root ginger
juice of 1 lime
50g (2oz) butter
about 1 tablespoon flour
1 heaped tablespoon curry powder
1 teaspoon ground cinnamon
150ml (5fl oz) coconut milk
1 bay leaf
1 tablespoon mango chutney
green coriander, to garnish

Joint the chicken and remove the skin. Cover the meat and refrigerate. Put the skin and chicken carcass in a stockpot with the onion skins, carrot, celery and black peppercorns, cover with water and simmer to make stock.

While this is cooking, make a seasoning paste: take one of the onions, one garlic clove, the turmeric, coriander, cayenne, sugar, salt and ginger and process them together in a blender. Add a little of the lime juice if it seems dry.

Melt the butter in a large pan. Dust the chicken pieces lightly with flour and fry until pale gold. Drain and set aside. Add the sliced onions and remaining garlic clove (crushed) and fry briskly. Stir frequently and cook until golden. Stir in the curry powder and allow to cook for a moment, then add the seasoning paste and cinnamon. Fry gently for a few minutes before stirring in about 150ml (5fl oz) chicken stock and 100ml (3½fl oz) coconut milk. Simmer for 15 minutes. Next add the bay leaf, the chutney and the remainder of the lime juice. Add the chicken pieces, bring to the boil and simmer very gently until the chicken is tender and cooked through – about 45 minutes, depending on the size of the pieces. Stir occasionally and add a little more stock if it shows signs of drying out.

Once the chicken is cooked, stir in the remaining coconut milk. Taste and adjust the seasoning if necessary. Garnish with coriander leaves and serve with rice.

Devilled Chicken

about 250g (9oz) cooked chicken
2 teaspoons Dijon mustard
½ teaspoon English mustard
  (made up, not powder)
½ teaspoon salt

2 heaped dessertspoons mango
  chutney – any large pieces of fruit
  in the chutney chopped fine
cayenne pepper, to taste
freshly ground black pepper

Prepare the chicken, pulling it into long, narrow pieces. The skin can be left on, as it crisps nicely under the grill. Mix the mustards, salt and chutney, adding as much cayenne as you feel desirable (try ¼ teaspoon if unsure) and a generous grind of black pepper. Rub the paste into the chicken pieces and leave in a cool place for 1–2 hours.

To cook, put the pieces under a preheated moderate grill for a few minutes. Keep a close eye on them and turn a couple of times, until they are well heated through. Any skin should turn quite crisp, and the edges of the pieces may brown, but try not to let them char. Alternatively, put them in a single layer in an ovenproof dish and bake in a hot oven, 220°C, 425°F, Gas mark 7, for 7–10 minutes.

Serve hot with rice and more chutney, or scatter over a salad of mixed leaves.

Fricassée of Chicken and Asparagus

1 chicken weighing about 1.5kg
(3lb 4oz)
zest and juice of 1 lemon
leaves of 4–6 large sprigs fresh thyme
1 tablespoon chopped parsley
30g (1oz) butter
1 small onion, peeled and finely
chopped

1 generous tablespoon flour
250ml (9fl oz) good chicken stock
2 bunches asparagus, washed, the
woody ends of the stems discarded
and the rest cut into pieces about
2cm (¾in) long
75ml (3fl oz) single cream
salt and black pepper

Cut the legs away from the body of the chicken and divide them into thigh and drumstick. Cut the breasts and wings off the bird. Divide each in two, leaving a portion of breast meat attached to each wing. Trim the tips off the wings. Skin the joints, putting the skin and carcass in the stockpot.

Mix together the lemon zest and juice, thyme and parsley. Grind in a generous amount of black pepper. Put the chicken into this mixture, turn it to coat well, then cover and leave to marinate for at least 2 hours (overnight if possible). Stir the meat around in the marinade from time to time.

To start the fricassée off, melt the butter in a frying pan and cook the onion gently until transparent. Lift it out and put it into a flameproof casserole or large pan. Remove the chicken from the marinade (reserve any remaining juices). Dust the joints with flour and brown them lightly in the butter used for frying the onions. Add them to the casserole or pan. Add any remaining flour into the frying pan, stir well to mop up any fat, and add about two-thirds of the stock and any leftover marinade. Stir well, scraping up any residues from frying and bring to the boil. Season with ½ teaspoon salt and pour over the chicken. Cover, and simmer over a very low heat for about 1 hour, or until the chicken pieces are cooked through. If it seems to be drying up, add a little more stock, but don't overdo it.

Allow the stew to cool a little and skim off any excess fat. Add the asparagus and return to the heat for 5–10 minutes, until the asparagus is just cooked. Add the cream, stir gently and heat through. Taste, adjust the seasoning and serve with new potatoes or rice.

Chicken and Wild Mushrooms
in a Potato Case

The idea for this recipe came from another of Colonel Kenny-Herbert's recipes, in this case the suggestion of serving *chicken à la financière* in small drum-shaped cases made of deep fried potato. Chicken cooked this way, is, as the name suggests, a rich production and the original requires large quantities of truffles. Though still quite complex to make, this recipe is more modest. If the idea of the enclosing potato case is daunting, serve the stew separately, with the mash baked in a buttered dish and scattered with the crumbs and cheese as an accompaniment.

<table>
<tr><td>serves
4</td><td>

1 chicken weighing about
   2–2.5kg (4lb 8oz–5lb 8oz)
1 carrot, trimmed and peeled
1 onion, peeled
1 celery stick
a bouquet garni of a bay leaf, some
   thyme and some parsley stems
10g (¼oz) dried porcini mushrooms
30g (1oz) butter
50g (2oz) pancetta (unsmoked),
   cut into matchsticks
400g (14oz) mushrooms (half button
   mushrooms and half chanterelles),
   washed and trimmed

</td><td>

30g (1oz) flour
100ml (3½fl oz) dry sherry
salt and black pepper

For the case

1.5kg (3lb 4oz) floury potatoes,
   peeled and cut into chunks
4 egg yolks
1 teaspoon salt
½ teaspoon mace
20g (¾oz) butter
20g (¾oz) breadcrumbs, made
   from stale bread
20g (¾oz) grated Parmesan

</td></tr>
</table>

You will need a deep round ovenproof dish or tin 20cm (8in) in diameter.

Begin with the chicken. Joint it, and cut the meat from the breasts and thighs into neat cubes. Cover the meat and keep in the fridge. Put the bones and the skin in a pan with the carrot, onion, celery and bouquet garni. Cover with water, bring to the boil and simmer gently for about 2 hours to make a good stock (use the wings and drumsticks for another dish, or add them to the stock pot). Strain off the stock, skim off as much fat as possible, then return 500ml (18fl oz) of it to a clean pan. Put this over gentle heat and allow it to reduce to about one-third of the original volume. This will be needed for the stew.

When ready to make the stew, put the dried mushrooms in a small bowl and add about 100ml (3½fl oz) boiling water. Then melt the butter in a frying pan and add the pancetta. Allow to cook gently until the fat is transparent. Remove and set aside. Slice the mushrooms and fry in the fat from cooking the bacon, cooking quite briskly and stirring frequently until they begin to brown. Drain and add to the pancetta.

Dust the chicken meat with flour and fry in the same pan, turning until lightly browned on all sides. Sprinkle in any remaining flour, stirring to absorb any fat in the pan, then add the sherry and let it bubble. Stir in the porcini and their soaking liquid, plus the fried mushrooms and pancetta. Add the reduced stock and mix well. Allow to cook very gently for about 30 minutes, by which time the chicken pieces should be well done. Taste and add salt and pepper as necessary.

For the potato case, boil the potatoes and mash (without additions). They are best passed through a ricer, a sieve or a mouli-legumes to make sure they are perfectly smooth. Beat in the egg yolks, salt and the mace, then return to the pan and stir them over a low heat for a few minutes to dry the mixture out a little.

Take the tin or dish and use some of the butter to coat the inside. Use two-thirds of the potato mixture to line the base and sides, covering them as evenly as possible and making sure there are no gaps or thin patches through which the stew can escape. Pour in the stew, ensuring that it doesn't come above the level of the potato lining. Carefully dot the rest of the potato over the top, then use a fork to spread it evenly across to form a lid and seal the edges. Melt the remaining butter and stir into the breadcrumbs. Add the Parmesan and sprinkle this mixture over the top of the potato.

Bake at 200°C, 400°F, Gas mark 6 for about 25 minutes, until the top is golden brown and the stew thoroughly hot. Unmould on to a deep dish if you feel brave; otherwise, serve from the cooking dish.

Chicken with Prunes & Saffron Broth

A simple but well-flavoured light stew based loosely on the Scottish cock-a-leekie, which involves a chicken and a piece of beef cooked in broth with prunes and leeks. I've omitted the beef and leeks from this recipe. Use a good-quality chicken; this can be cooked whole in the broth and carved afterwards if desired, but it is easier to handle if cut into joints.

serves
4

12 ready-to-eat prunes
2 tablespoons whisky (optional)
400ml (14fl oz) strong chicken stock
12 whole peppercorns
a pinch of saffron threads

1 sprig parsley
1 chicken, about 1.5–2kg
    (3lb 4oz–4lb 8oz), cut into
    four joints
salt

The evening before you want to make the stew, put the prunes into a small bowl with the whisky and turn them around in it. If you don't want to use whisky, omit this step and proceed as below.

When ready to cook, put the stock into a large pan and add the prunes plus any whisky they haven't soaked up, the peppercorns, saffron and sprig of parsley. Bring to a simmer, add the chicken pieces, season with 1 scant teaspoon salt and cover. Simmer gently for 30–40 minutes, or until the chicken pieces are cooked all the way through.

Serve each joint in a deep plate, adding a generous amount of broth and two or three prunes to each helping. Boiled floury potatoes, or potatoes mashed with cooked leeks are good accompaniments to the stew.

Chicken in Red Wine

This recipe, based on the French *coq au vin*, is reminiscent of rich, meaty 18th-century ragoos and chickens cooked *à la braise*. True *coq au vin* is difficult to make properly without the vital ingredient – a cockerel weighing in at several kilos, with richly flavoured dense meat that needs slow cooking; however, a good free-range chicken and careful preparation and seasoning gives a delicious stew, well worth the effort.

serves
4 – 6

150g (5½oz) fat bacon or pancetta (unsmoked), cut into 1cm (½in) dice
about 16 small shallots or button onions, peeled
250g (9oz) mushrooms (small open ones with dark gills are best)
about 20g (¾oz) butter
a chicken weighing about 2kg (4lb 8oz), cut into 8 joints
1 medium onion, peeled and chopped

1 medium carrot, trimmed, peeled and chopped
4 garlic cloves, peeled and crushed
100ml (3½fl oz) brandy
1 bottle red wine (Burgundy for preference)
1 bay leaf
3–4 sprigs thyme
1 teaspoon concentrated beef stock
salt and black pepper

Fry the bacon or pancetta until most of the fat has been given up and the pieces are quite crisp. Remove and set aside. Put the button onions in the fat, fry until they colour and add to the bacon pieces. Fry the mushrooms until the tops turn gold in patches and add to the bacon and onions. Add the butter to the remaining bacon fat and fry the chicken, skin-side down, until gold. Put to one side.

Add the onion, carrot and garlic to the pan and cook, stirring frequently, until the onion turns gold. Warm the brandy in a ladle, ignite it and pour into the pan, stirring well. When the flames have died down, add the wine. Add the bay leaf, thyme and stock, bring to the boil, and then cook rapidly until reduced by half.

Remove the herbs, cool a little and blitz in a blender or food processor. Transfer to a casserole. Add the chicken, mushrooms, onion and bacon, black pepper and ½ teaspoon salt. Cook in the oven for 40 minutes at 180°C, 350°F, Gas mark 4, stirring halfway through. Check that the thickest parts of the chicken are fully cooked (if still a little pink, cook for a few more minutes).

Chicken and Leek Pie

Chicken makes an excellent pie filling. In the traditions of the English kitchen, it is often combined with ham, as is veal; mushrooms are another common addition. Leeks are less usual, but they make a good winter pie.

serves 4

1 chicken
50g (2oz) flour, plus extra for dusting
scrape of nutmeg
50g (2oz) butter
a piece of lean ham or gammon,
   weighing about 200g (7oz),
   cut into about 1cm (½in) cubes

4–6 leeks (depending on size), white
   part only, washed and cut into
   1cm (½in) lengths
300ml (10fl oz) chicken stock
1 quantity puff pastry (see page 25)
beaten egg, cream or milk to glaze
salt and black pepper

Joint and skin the bird as directed in Fricassée of Chicken and Asparagus (see page 150). Season the flour with ½ teaspoon salt, some pepper and a good scrape of nutmeg. Dust the chicken joints with the mixture. Melt the butter in a large frying pan and brown the chicken lightly. Put the ham or gammon into the base of a suitable pie dish. Put the chicken on top, and then the sliced leeks.

Stir any remaining flour into the butter left in the pan, then stir in the chicken stock. Bring to the boil, stirring all the time, and cook for a few minutes. Taste to check the seasoning and add a little more if necessary. Pour this into the pie dish as well. Allow to cool a little.

Cover the pie with the pastry (see page 24). Decorate with pastry leaves, as taste and fancy suggest, and glaze with beaten egg, cream or milk.

Bake in a hot oven, 220°C, 425°F, Gas mark 7, for 20 minutes to set the pastry, then reduce the heat to 180°C, 350°F, Gas mark 4 and cook for a further 45–50 minutes until the pastry is golden and the filling cooked through.

Coronation Chicken

Devised for the coronation of Queen Elizabeth II in 1953, this could be regarded as a variation on the theme of chicken mayonnaise. The industrial versions used as sandwich fillings in the 1990s did few favours for what is, when well made, a delicious dish, which most people love.

serves
4–6

2 tablespoons sunflower oil
1 small onion, peeled and very finely chopped
1 dessertspoon curry powder (mild Madras)
generous 1 tablespoon mango chutney, rubbed through a sieve
250g (9oz) mayonnaise, home-made or good-quality bottled

1 cold roast chicken, skinned, boned and divided into neat, roughly bite-sized chunks
flaked almonds, toasted until golden brown
salt and pepper
lettuce leaves, lightly dressed with oil and vinegar, to serve

Heat the oil and fry the onion very gently until translucent. Stir in the curry powder and continue to cook gently until it loses its raw smell. Remove from the heat and allow to cool.

Stir in the mango chutney and the mayonnaise to make a thick, lightly curried cold sauce. Taste and adjust the seasoning. Arrange the chicken pieces on top of the lettuce leaves and pour the curried mayonnaise over. Scatter the almonds on top.

Roast Guinea Fowl

Recipes for roasting guinea fowl – or guinea-hens, as they were sometimes called – appear from the 19th century onwards; the English usually seem to have treated the birds simply, regarding them in the same light as pheasants. They can be tricky to cook well, as the meat on the breast tends to cook through and dry out before the legs are fully cooked. Starting the bird on its side for 15 minutes, then turning it on to the other side for another 15 minutes, before finally turning it on to its back overcomes this to some extent.

serves 3–4

unsalted butter
2–4 rashers fat bacon
   (unsmoked streaky is best)
1 guinea fowl, about 1kg (2¼lb)

100ml (3½fl oz) port (optional)
150ml (5fl oz) well-flavoured
   chicken stock
salt and pepper

Lightly butter a small roasting tin in which the guinea fowl will fit nicely. Wrap the bacon around the breast of the bird and tie on with string.

Preheat the oven to 200°C, 400°F, Gas mark 6. Roast the bird for 20 minutes at this temperature, then reduce the heat to 180°C, 350°F, Gas mark 4 and cook for a further 25 minutes. Then remove the bacon, season with a little salt and continue to roast until the juices run clear. Allow to rest for about 10 minutes before serving.

To make the gravy, pour off all the cooking juices into a bowl and skim off and discard the fat that rises to the surface. Deglaze the roasting dish with the port, if using, or the chicken stock. Add the cooking juices and boil hard to produce a fairly small amount of thin, well-flavoured gravy. Adjust the seasoning with salt and pepper as necessary.

To accompany a guinea fowl, serve Bread Sauce (page 39). A salad of watercress was favoured as an accompaniment by 19th-century cookery authors, but, writing in 1905, Colonel Kenney-Herbert suggested a salad of cos lettuce that was dressed with some wine vinegar, olive oil, and a seasoning of 1 teaspoon each of chopped tarragon and chives.

The Italian Way of Roasting a Turkey

4.5kg (10lb) oven-ready turkey
about 30g (1oz) unsalted butter
2–3 rashers unsmoked bacon
1 large carrot, chopped
1 onion, peeled and chopped
1 small white turnip, chopped
2 celery sticks, chopped
3 garlic cloves, peeled and chopped
2 large fresh rosemary sprigs
4–5 cloves
500ml (18fl oz) giblet or chicken stock
1–2 tablespoons arrowroot
salt

For the stuffing
unsalted butter
about 100g (4oz) unsmoked
    bacon, rind removed, chopped
    in small pieces
about 100g (4oz) good-quality
    sausage meat
100g (4oz) chestnut purée
3 prunes, pitted and chopped
1 small hard pear, peeled
    and chopped
75ml (3fl oz) Marsala
salt and pepper

Make the stuffing: melt the butter, add the bacon and sausage meat, and fry gently for a few minutes. Stir in the chestnut purée, prunes, pear and Marsala, and season with a little salt and plenty of pepper. Cool and use to stuff the crop.

To cook the turkey, use a stout roasting tin. Smear the butter over the base, and put the bacon and vegetables in. Add the garlic, rosemary and cloves. Put in the turkey on its back, and add stock to cover the base of the tin. Season. Cover the whole with a sheet of tinfoil, crimping it firmly. Put the tin on the hob on the lowest heat. Braise the bird, gently, for about 1½ hours. Check occasionally, adding more liquid if necessary.

Preheat the oven to 180–190°C, 350–375°F, Gas mark 4–5. Move the turkey, still in the covered container, into the oven, and cook for another 45–60 minutes. Remove the foil, baste well, salt the skin and roast, uncovered, for 45 minutes. Add a little liquid if the juices look dry. When cooked, allow to rest. Tip what's left in the tin through a sieve, catching the juices in a bowl. Press with the back of a wooden spoon to extract any liquid. Put the juices in a pan. Add about 250ml (9fl oz) stock. Finish by slaking the arrowroot with a little cold water; stir this into the gravy and reheat until just boiling and lightly thickened.

Turkey Pie

Turkey, chicken or veal and ham combinations are all traditional in pies in English cookery. Add some mushrooms, or make a particularly good (if expensive) version by adding some of the white truffle and porcini paste sold in jars in Italian delicatessens.

serves 4–6

40g (1½oz) unsalted butter
150g (5oz) button mushrooms, sliced
40g (1½oz) plain flour
350ml (12fl oz) well-flavoured turkey stock
shortcrust pastry made with 100g (4oz) unsalted butter and lard mixed, and 200g (7oz) plain flour

40g (1½oz) white truffle and porcini paste (optional)
200–250g (7–9oz) cooked turkey, cut in neat pieces
125g (4½oz) cooked ham or gammon, cut in dice
1 medium egg, beaten
salt and pepper

Melt the butter in a saucepan and cook the mushrooms until all the liquid they exude has evaporated, but don't allow them to brown. Stir in the flour to make a roux, then add the stock gradually, stirring to produce a sauce. Season to taste and allow to cool.

When ready to bake, preheat the oven to 200°C, 400°F, Gas mark 6, and put a metal baking sheet in to heat.

Roll two-thirds of the pastry fairly thin and use it to line a pie dish about 20cm (8in) in diameter.

If using the truffle paste, mix it with the turkey meat. Distribute this, and the ham, over the pastry. Spoon the sauce in on top. Roll out the remaining pastry and use to cover the pie, sealing and crimping the edges. Cut a hole in the top for the steam to escape and decorate the surface of the pie with leaves made from the pastry trimmings. Brush with beaten egg.

Put the pie on the preheated baking sheet and cook for 15–20 minutes to set and crisp the pastry. Then reduce the heat to 180°C, 350°F, Gas mark 4, and bake for a further 20–25 minutes. Serve hot or cold.

Alderman in Chains

serves 8

1 oven-ready turkey, about 4.5–5kg
   (10–11lb)
75g (3oz) unsalted butter, softened
8 sausages in a string
splash of or chicken stock,
   to deglaze
1–2 tablespoons arrowroot

For the green herb stuffing
150g (5oz) stale breadcrumbs

1 dessertspoon finely chopped fresh
   thyme or marjoram leaves
1 tablespoon finely chopped parsley
grated zest of ½ lemon (preferably
   unwaxed)
75g (3oz) beef suet, or unsalted
   butter broken into small pieces
1–2 medium eggs, beaten
1 teaspoon salt
freshly ground black pepper

For the stuffing, mix all ingredients together, adding the eggs last, to give a soft mixture. Use this to stuff the crop of the turkey, then sew the skin closed over it.

Preheat the oven to 170°C, 325°F, Gas mark 3. Calculate the roasting time (see page 138). Spread the softened butter over the bird and season well. Place it on one side in the roasting tin. Cook for about 45 minutes, basting it every 15 minutes. Turn it on to the other side and baste well, then cook for another 45 minutes. Turn it on to its back and baste again, then protect the breast with a piece of foil and continue to cook, basting regularly.

About 45 minutes before the end of cooking time, put the sausages into a baking tray (don't cut the links) and put them in the oven to cook. About 15 minutes before the end of cooking time, remove the foil and allow the skin to brown. When the bird is fully cooked, rest for 20 minutes. Check the sausages, keeping them in a string.

Skim off any fat from the cooking juices and add the stock. Bring to the boil, scraping the tin. Mix the arrowroot with a little cold water and add to the juices. Heat gently until the arrowroot has become translucent and thickened the gravy.

Present the bird with the string of cooked sausages draped over the breast of the bird or around its front – the 'chains' of the pouting alderman.

Braised Turkey and Celery with Tarragon Dumplings

The combination of turkey and celery is a neglected classic of the English kitchen. Maybe this is because 19th-century versions requiring a whole boiled turkey and a sauce based on several heads of celery look daunting, but the combination works well in a less grand manner.

serves
4

20g (¾oz) butter
4 small shallots, peeled and
    finely chopped
400–500g (14oz–1lb 2oz) turkey
    thigh, diced
20g (¾oz) flour
2–3 sprigs lemon thyme
zest of ½ lemon
about ½ teaspoon ground mace
400ml (14fl oz) strong turkey or
    chicken stock
salt and black pepper

½ head celery trimmed and cut into
    2cm (¾in) lengths

For the dumplings
120g (4oz) plain flour, plus a little
    for dusting
80g (3¼oz) white breadcrumbs
1 teaspoon baking powder
a generous pinch salt
100g (3½oz) suet
1 tablespoon chopped tarragon
about 200ml (7fl oz) water

Melt the butter in a heavy frying pan. Add the shallots and cook gently for about 10 minutes, or until translucent. Toss the turkey meat in flour and fry until the outside is lightly coloured. Add the thyme, lemon zest and mace, then stir in the stock. Season with 1 scant teaspoon salt and a little pepper and add the celery. Bring to a simmer, transfer to a casserole, cover and cook in the oven at 160°C, 325°F, Gas mark 3 for about 1 hour.

Towards the end of this time, make the dumpling mixture: put everything except the water in a bowl and mix well. Add the water gradually, stirring until it forms a soft, slightly sticky dough (add a little more water if necessary). Dust a board and your fingers with flour and form the dough into about 18–20 dumplings.

By now, the meat should be just cooked but not yet tender. Skim off any excess fat, taste and season. Put the dumplings on the stew and return to the oven, uncovered, for another 20–30 minutes, or until they are crisp on top and golden.

Turkey Fricassée

A simple, soothing dish using the wine-flavoured creamy sauce typical of fricassées of the late 18th and early 19th centuries. Truffle paste can be bought in small jars and, while not cheap, is a relatively inexpensive method for adding concentrated mushroom flavour to dishes of this type.

serves
4

20g (¾oz) butter
500g (1lb 2oz) turkey breast meat, cut
   into strips
1 garlic clove, peeled but left whole
60–80ml (2–2¾fl oz) white wine
60–80ml (2–2¾fl oz) single cream

2 generous teaspoons truffle paste
2 teaspoons butter kneaded
   with 2 teaspoons flour
salt and black pepper
chopped parsley, to garnish

Melt the butter in a frying pan that has a lid. Add the turkey meat and brown lightly on both sides. Put in the garlic clove, then stir in the wine and let it bubble. Season with ½ teaspoon salt and some black pepper. Cover, reduce the heat and allow the mixture to cook gently for about 10 minutes or until the meat is done. Remove the garlic.

Stir in the cream and bring back to the boil for a couple of minutes. Add the truffle paste and stir well. Check the seasoning. Dot the flour and butter mixture over the surface of the sauce and shake the pan so that it melts in and thickens it slightly (it may not all be needed).

Garnish with chopped parsley and serve with rice or pasta.

Daube of Turkey

Daube is a word now applied to a dish of meat and vegetables braised slowly. This old-fashioned dish of French farmhouse cookery uses specially shaped pots, which are bulbous with narrow necks. They hold the ingredients in layers and the small opening cuts down on evaporation. Any deep pot will do. Ask the butcher for a piece of pork rind – this adds body and richness to the sauce. Chorizo is not traditional, but goes well with turkey.

serves
4

turkey breast steaks, weighing about
   100–125g (3½oz–4½oz) each
a thin rasher of bacon for each steak
100g (3½oz) pork rind, cut in
   small pieces
1 medium onion, peeled and
   finely chopped
4–6 small shallots, peeled and
   finely chopped
1 medium carrot, peeled and
   cut in small dice

1 beef tomato, skin and seeds
   removed, flesh diced
1 clove garlic, peeled and crushed
100g (3½oz) chorizo sausage, cut
   in thick slices
a bouquet garni of a piece of leek,
   celery, 1 bay leaf, a few sprigs
   of thyme and parsley and a strip
   of orange zest
400ml (14fl oz) white wine
salt and black pepper

Wrap each piece of turkey in a rasher of bacon. Blanch the pork rind by putting it in a small pan, adding boiling water and cooking for 2–3 minutes. Drain it. Mix the onion, shallot, carrot, tomato and garlic together.

Put the pork rind into the pot and add a layer of vegetables. Put the chorizo sausage on top and scatter more vegetables over. Put the bacon-wrapped turkey steaks on top of this and add the bouquet garni. Season with some pepper and about ½ teaspoon salt (the sausage and bacon will also be salty, so be cautious). Cover with the remaining vegetables and pour in the wine.

Put the lid on the pot with a layer of foil underneath to make it airtight. Transfer to a low oven, 140°C, 275°F, Gas mark 1, for 2½–3 hours.

This can be eaten hot or allowed to cool in the pot and for gentle re-heating. If the sauce seems thin, pour some into a small pan and reduce by fast boiling before returning it to the stew.

Roast Goose

Goose has a skin that crisps up wonderfully on cooking. For optimum results, use a boiling water treatment similar to that for pork crackling (see page 69). About 6–12 hours before cooking, remove the goose from any packaging and stand it on a rack over the sink. Prick the skin, especially the parts that have fat deposits underneath. Boil a large kettleful of water and pour over the bird (turn it so that both back and front get the treatment). Pat dry very thoroughly with kitchen paper. Also dry the inside, taking especial care in the neck area, which tends to contain blood clots – wipe to get rid of these. Then put the goose in a cool airy place, or in the refrigerator; cover lightly with greaseproof paper or a clean tea towel. Geese are large birds and the amount of fat they yield during cooking is startling. Make sure the oven is big enough. You will need a deep roasting tin, a rack, a pair of sturdy oven gloves, and a capacious bowl for the fat. A supply of heavy-duty tinfoil is also useful. Allow 30 minutes per 500g.

serves
6

1 goose
stuffing, as required
giblet stock

2 tablespoons arrowroot
salt and pepper

About 1 hour before you want to start cooking the bird, allow it to come to room temperature. Preheat the oven to 220°C, 425°F, Gas mark 7. Rub the bird with salt and pepper and stuff the body. Place the goose on a rack in a deep roasting tin. Start it breast downwards. Use tinfoil to extend the tin under any of the goose that projects over the edge (it's also useful for wrapping round wing tips and ends of drumsticks if they show signs of browning too fast).

Put the goose into the oven and cook for 30 minutes, then turn the heat down to 180–190°C, 350–375°F, Gas mark 4–5 and continue to roast. After 30 minutes, remove from the oven and carefully ladle the fat out of the roasting tin into a bowl. Turn the goose on to its back. Return it to the oven and continue to cook. Keep checking the fat in the roasting tin, and pour it off into a bowl from time to time. When cooked, rest for about 20 minutes.

To finish the gravy, pour off the fat, returning any browned cooking juices and sediment to the tin. Pour in the giblet stock, stir to deglaze, and bring to the boil. Slake the arrowroot with a little water and pour into the gravy. Bring it back to boiling point to thicken. Check the seasoning, then strain into a gravy boat.

Slow-Roast Duck Legs
with Marmalade

The orange flavourings can also be used to marinate portions of duck.

serves
4

4 duck legs
1 generous tablespoon bitter orange
   marmalade
juice of 1 (sweet) orange
juice of 1 lemon
a little stock (optional)
salt and pepper

Put the duck legs in an ovenproof dish that holds them neatly. Mix the marmalade, orange and lemon juices, and pour over the duck. Cover and then leave in the refrigerator to marinate for 24 hours. Stir from time to time to make sure the duck is well coated with marinade.

Cook the duck legs at 140°C, 275°F, Gas mark 1 for 1¾ hours, turning them after 1 hour. About 15 minutes before the end of cooking time, pour the fat and cooking juices into a bowl and turn up the heat to 170°C, 325°F, Gas mark 3 to crisp the skin.

When the duck legs are ready, remove them to a serving plate. Skim the fat off the reserved cooking juices and use the latter to deglaze the roasting dish (you may want to add a little stock or water to help the process along, but don't overdo it – there should be a relatively small quantity of thin, concentrated gravy). Taste, adjust the seasoning, and serve.

Stewed Duck with Green Peas

Recorded from the early 18th century onwards, stewed duck and green peas became a classic of English summer food. Success depends on good stock, which must be well flavoured. If in doubt about this, start with about half as much again, add a little onion, carrot, parsley and some mushroom trimmings and allow it to reduce gently to the amount required. Beef stock or gravy was always specified for this dish.

serves
4

30g (1oz) butter
1 duck, jointed, or 4 duck joints
flour, for dusting
100g (3½oz) pancetta or bacon
    cut into matchsticks
8 small shallots, peeled and halved
2 tablespoons brandy
a bouquet garni of parsley, thyme,
    1 bay leaf and 1 sprig mint
zest of ½ lemon, cut into thin strips
3–4 cloves, pounded to a powder
a pinch of cayenne

350ml (12fl oz) well-flavoured
    beef stock
200g (7oz) frozen peas
4–6 spring onions, trimmed
    and finely sliced
leaves from 6–8 sprigs mint, finely
    chopped – about 1 generous
    tablespoon
leaves from 6–8 sprigs basil,
    torn into shreds
salt

Melt the butter in a wide pan. Dust the duck with flour, then brown slowly on both sides in the butter. Remove from the pan; pour off the fat.

Return the pan to a low heat. Spread the pancetta or bacon and shallots over the base. Put the duck on top, then pour in the brandy and let it bubble away. Add the bouquet garni, lemon zest, 1 scant teaspoon salt, the cloves and cayenne. Pour in the stock, bring to a simmer and cover. Let the mixture stew very gently for about 1 hour. Towards the end of this time, test the duck meat to see if it is cooked – the juices should run clear. When done, transfer the pieces to a serving dish. Discard the bouquet garni. Skim off the excess fat.

Return the pan with the cooking juices to the heat. Add the peas and spring onions and bring to the boil. Season if necessary. As soon as the peas are done, remove from the heat, stir in the mint and basil and serve with a bowl of little new potatoes.

Game Birds

GAME IS OUR COLLECTIVE TERM FOR WILD ANIMALS and birds that are hunted. It encompasses a wide range – from very small birds suitable for one portion, such as snipe, up to large beasts such as red deer. The game birds in Britain are pheasant, partridge, grouse, pigeon, woodcock, snipe and several species of wild duck. Game animals include rabbit, hare and deer (see page 188), most importantly red, fallow and roe deer. In recent years, wild boar have also been reintroduced to Britain as farmed animals.

Since the Middle Ages, there has always been some management of game species. Methods have included controlling predators and encouraging specific environments, such as grouse moors. Pheasants are reared and fed in such large numbers for shoots that they are now semi-domesticated. Game is a category of food with blurred boundaries. What probably would have surprised our ancestors is the relative cheapness and wide availability of certain types, especially pheasants. Since the Norman Conquest, much energy has been devoted to protecting large areas of land as hunting preserves. The consumption of meat from wild birds and animals found on these lands was restricted to the aristocracy (hence the art of the poacher). This restriction made game birds sought after as a food for grand meals and large feasts, having a far higher status than beef, mutton and pork.

Once upon a time, the category of game birds included a much wider range than that now available or eaten. They featured at great feasts, together with exotic domestic fowl such as peacocks. Birds that appeared on the table included herons, bustards, bittern, curlews, plover and numerous small birds no longer considered as food in Britain.

The good flavour of game birds was prized for stock-making in the kitchens of the past. In the 18th century, partridges were often added to the general brew of meats for the rich gravies and meat coulis that seem to have flavoured or accompanied almost every meat at the table. In the 19th century, birds were often used as a basis for consommé. Older birds, unsuitable for presenting as roasts, were employed for such dishes. Methods for roasting, however, always seem to have been plain and unadorned.

The presentation of game birds at table has changed over the centuries. Our ancestors expected to find various extremities still in place. Tastes seem to have changed in the early 19th century: in a precursor of a sentiment now widespread, Eliza Acton commented that pheasant 'was formerly always sent to the table with the head on, but it was a barbarous custom, which has been partially abandoned of late in the best houses, and which it is hoped may soon be altogether superseded by one of better taste'.

Pheasants can be extremely cheap (especially if you live near a large shoot and can dress them yourself). This is because pheasant chicks are often hatched indoors and given extra feed after they

---

are released into the woods, which has vastly increased their availability and decreased their price. Some game birds, however, remain very expensive – such as grouse, woodcock and snipe. They can also be expensive to buy. Game provides a variety of flavours and textures outside the variety of domestic birds, and meat that is very definitely free-range.

Buying game

All birds intended for roasting should be young ones. You will have to trust the game dealer, and buy earlier in the season rather than later. Game from the wild (except pigeon and rabbit) is also subject to laws restricting the times of year when it can be shot. The seasons when wild birds are available are as follows:

- pheasant: 1 October–1 February
- partridge: 1 September–1 February
- grouse: 12 August–10 December
- woodcock: 1 October–31 March
- snipe: 12 August–31 January

Hanging game develops the flavour and helps to tenderise the flesh. Birds are hung by the neck, complete with feathers and insides, in a cool, airy place. The length of time for which they should be hung depends on the weather (longer is required in cold weather) and is also, to some extent, a matter of taste. The old method of telling if a pheasant was sufficiently well hung was to try pulling one of the tail feathers: if it came out easily, the bird was judged to be at the correct stage. It is unlikely that a purchased pheasant would now be hung for more than 7–10 days, except by special request. Times for other birds differ: partridge and grouse need only 2–3 days. Hanging was also, in the days before freezing as a preservation method, a means of extending the season for game, as birds shot right at the end of the season could be kept for some time in really cold weather.

Buying game is something of a lottery. If some game birds are now relatively inexpensive, this is partly because they are prepared quickly, in large numbers and with the aid of machines. Unless you can buy game birds freshly shot and in the feathers, and are willing and able to pluck and dress them yourself, then only trial and error will show who prepares them the best.

A pheasant will serve 4 people. Allow one grey-legged partridge per person; a red-legged one may be larger, but it is still probably safer to allow one per person. Quail were once wild game birds but they azre now farmed – they belong to the partridge family. Allow 1–2 birds per person

Cooking game birds

The old expression relating to the cooking of small game birds and wild duck was that they 'should just fly through the kitchen'. Cookery books usually state that game birds, especially small ones like partridge, should be served rare (with the breast meat pink or just done). This is not to everyone's taste, and can leave the legs quite underdone. If you wish to serve the birds whole, then you may have to compromise: if you would like the legs to be cooked through, the breast meat will be more cooked with some risk of dryness; if you would like the breast meat to be just done, the legs may be very underdone. Resting the bird helps. Alternatively – although purists would frown on this – carve off the breasts from the birds after a short rest, return the birds to the oven for a few minutes, then carve the legs and serve piled up on a croûton.

Roasting times and temperatures

- Pheasants: start at 200°C, 400°F, Gas mark 6 for 20 minutes, then reduce to 180°C, 350°F, Gas mark 4 for 20–30 minutes. Don't overcook, as they become dry, tough and flavourless.
- Partridges: start at 200°C, 400°F, Gas mark 6 for 10 minutes, then reduce to 180°C, 350°F, Gas mark 4 for 10–15 minutes, or until done to taste. Partridges have a rich and distinctive flavour. There are two species available: the native grey-legged, and the slightly larger French red-legged partridge, a bird introduced to south-eastern England. Both make good eating, but they must be young for roasting, and the red-legged needs care to make sure it doesn't dry out.
- Quail: roast at 200°C, 400°F, Gas mark 6 for 20–25 minutes.

Roast game birds

Season inside and out, with salt and pepper. Add a squeeze of lemon juice to the body cavity. Bard with bacon or spread butter over the breast. Do not cover. Put the birds on their backs in a roasting tin just large enough to hold them. Roast according to the times and temperatures given above.

About 10 minutes before the end of cooking, remove any covering from the breast of the birds, baste well and dust with flour. When cooked to your liking (examine the colour of the flesh between the thigh and body of the bird to ascertain how well done they are), remove the birds to a hot serving dish and keep warm while you make the gravy.

Tip off as much fat as possible from the roasting tin. Add 1 teaspoon flour and stir over a gentle heat to cook and brown slightly. Stir in 250ml (9fl oz) well-flavoured chicken stock. Bring to the boil and cook gently for a few minutes. Check the seasoning. The gravy should be clear and thin.

Making stock from game bones

If all you have available is the leftovers from roasting a few partridge or a brace of pheasants, it is still possible to make stock. Collect all the bones, skin and debris of the birds and put in a suitable pan. The remains of 4 partridge will produce about 750ml (1¼ pints) of well-flavoured stock when finished. 3–4 tablespoons of sherry, port or wine will improve the stock – add it and heat till it boils, then add 1 litre (1¾ pints) of water. Also add a piece of onion; a few black peppercorns; a bouquet garni made of bay leaf, parsley stalks and thyme sprigs; a small carrot; and some ham trimmings if you have them. Simmer very gently for 1½–2 hours, topping up with fresh water if necessary, or use a slow cooker. Strain the stock, measure it and (if necessary) reduce by fast boiling. Venison bones can be used in the same way.

Cooking game birds in stews and casseroles

Because of their associations with hunting and landed estates, game birds have always had high status. Despite the abundance of pheasants wandering the country lanes, this past glory still clings to them, and they are given a certain amount of deference in the kitchen. Stewing was usually relegated to a method for cooking older, tougher birds, and it was the leftovers of roasts that were converted to hashes and little-made dishes.

The meat of all these birds is lean, although cooking in a sauce counteracts dryness. In the past, birds were generally larded and cooked whole, often with some kind of forcemeat as a stuffing. To make serving easier, you can joint pheasants before consigning them to the pot; remove the skins as well if you like. Smaller birds can be partially boned if you wish, cutting down the back and carefully working round the ribs and breastbones, then cutting through the wing and leg joints where they leave the body; put some forcemeat into the space and skewer or sew up the skin to return them to their former appearance. The carcasses can be used to make stock for the dish, and the birds are easier to deal with at the table.

Flavourings for stews and casseroles

All game birds are good with the rich wine sauces distantly derived from many 18th-century braised dishes (see Pheasant with Port and Chestnuts, page 179). Since pheasants, especially, have lost a little of their glory, a wider variety of stews is worth experimenting with, such as Pheasant with Spiced Sausage and Peppers (see page 180). Alternatively, take the meat off the bone and use instead of chicken in Chicken and Wild Mushrooms in a Potato Case (see page 152) or instead of venison in Venison and Mushroom Pie (see page 196). Partridges are also excellent in any dish with wild mushrooms.

Cooking times

Unless the birds are older than the current season (unlikely in these days of managed shoots) cooking times, even for gentle stewing, will not be long. Whole quail take about 25 minutes; partridge, 45 minutes to 1 hour; pheasants, a little longer.

Cooking game birds in pies

Any game birds can be made into a pie. A proper game pie was made traditionally with a raised crust to be eaten cold, but you can make hot pies with puff or shortcrust pastry.

Pheasant with Port and Chestnuts

A recipe that draws inspiration from the dishes *à la braise* from the 18th century. I've suggested leaving the pheasant whole, but for easier serving it can be cut into quarters before cooking.

serves
3–4

100g (3½oz) unsmoked bacon or
    pancetta, cut into cubes
1 pheasant, prepared as if for roasting
a little butter or oil – about
    2 tablespoons
200g (7oz) shallots, peeled and finely
    chopped
2 garlic cloves, peeled and crushed
8 juniper berries, crushed
100ml (3½fl oz) port

a bouquet garni of 1 sprig rosemary,
    2–3 sprigs parsley, 2–3 sprigs thyme
    and 2 bay leaves
200ml (7fl oz) strong beef or game
    stock
200g (7oz) cooked, peeled chestnuts
    (use canned or in vacuum packs)
1 tablespoon arrowroot (optional)
salt and black pepper

Preheat the oven to 150°C, 300°F, Gas mark 2. Heat a heavy, flameproof casserole and add the cubes of bacon or pancetta. Allow them to cook gently so that they brown slightly. When they have yielded their fat, remove them with a slotted spoon and keep on one side. Brown the pheasant in the fat, turning it so that all sides colour slightly. Remove and put it with the bacon or pancetta.

If necessary, add a little butter or oil to the casserole with the shallots and garlic. Cook gently until softened. Stir in the juniper berries and port and let it bubble. Add the bacon and pheasant, then put in the bouquet garni and the stock.

Bring to the boil, cover with foil and the lid, and cook in the oven for 1 hour, then test to check that the bird is cooked: a tender young bird may be done by this point, but if you like the meat well done, it may need another 30 minutes, and an older bird takes longer. Stir in the chestnuts during the last 10 minutes of cooking; since they are pre-prepared, they only need to be heated through.

When it is done, taste the gravy and aseason to taste. For a thickened gravy, strain the cooking juices into a small pan. Skim and discard any excess fat. Mix the arrowroot with a little water and stir into the gravy. Bring to the boil to give a glossy, thickened sauce. Carve the pheasant and serve with the sauce.

Roast Pheasant
with Pancetta and Lemon

serves 3–4

1 pheasant
1 lemon
75g (3oz) pancetta, thinly sliced
unsalted butter

1 teaspoon plain flour
150ml (5fl oz) stock made from the
  giblets of the bird, or from
  chicken or veal

Skin the pheasant. Preheat the oven to 200°C, 400°F, Gas mark 6.

Peel the lemon by cutting off each end, then standing it on a board, and slicing the peel off in vertical strips, taking off zest, skin and pith together. Cut the lemon across in the thinnest possible slices, removing any pips as you go.

Lay the pheasant on its back and cover the breast and upper surface with the lemon slices. Swaddle it up in pancetta, overlapping the slices where necessary. Take a piece of string, pass it under the back of the bird about halfway down the wings, then bring it up over the breast in a cross and back under in another cross somewhere near the middle of the thighs and finally up again, tying it neatly.

Lightly butter a roasting tin and put the pheasant in on its back. Roast, checking occasionally to make sure the pancetta isn't browning too much; if it is darkening a lot, turn the heat down slightly and roast for a little longer. After 20 minutes, reduce the heat to 180°C, 350°F, Gas mark 4 and roast for 20–30 minutes. Test for done-ness with a skewer pushed into the thickest part of the leg; if the juices run clear, or with only a slight hint of pink, it is done.

Remove the pheasant to a warmed serving dish and cut away the string. Pour the juices from the roasting tin into a small bowl and skim off the fat, returning about a dessertspoon to the tin. Sprinkle in the flour, then stir in the juices and mix to a paste. Add the stock, bit by bit, stirring constantly and bring to the boil; you should have a thin, well-flavoured gravy. Remove the pancetta (which should be crisp) just before carving, and serve.

Pheasant with Spiced Sausage and Peppers

This recipe is old-fashioned in the sense that it is based on one first published 60 years ago, by Elizabeth David in her book *French Provincial Cookery* (1960). This dish is very different to standard game recipes, and well worth trying out.

serves 4–6

2 tablespoons butter, duck or goose fat
1 pheasant, jointed into 8 pieces
about 1 tablespoon flour, for dusting
140g (4½oz) unsmoked pancetta
 or bacon, in one piece
12 small shallots, peeled
4 garlic cloves, peeled
2 tablespoons brandy
1 fresh red chilli (optional), strings
 and seeds removed, cut into fine
 slices or tiny dice

a bouquet garni of several sprigs
 oregano, thyme, parsley and a
 couple of strips of orange zest
200g (7oz) Spanish chorizo sausage,
 cut into 1cm (½in) lengths
1 red pepper, strings and seeds
 removed, cut into 1cm (½in) dice
1 yellow pepper, strings and seeds
 removed, cut into 1cm (½in) dice
200ml (7fl oz) game or chicken
 stock

Melt the butter or fat in an flameproof casserole. Pat the pheasant joints dry, then shake the flour over them. Brown them quickly in the fat and set aside.

Cut the pancetta or bacon into dice about 1cm (½in) square and add them to the fat. Cook fairly briskly, stirring from time to time, until the fat is translucent. Add the shallots and continue to cook, stirring, so that they start to brown in places. Stir in the garlic cloves and cook a moment longer.

Warm the brandy in a ladle, let it catch light and pour over the bacon mixture. Shake the dish until the flames die down, then return the pheasant to the pan. Add the chilli if using, and the bouquet garni. Put the chorizo on top, then the peppers. Pour in the stock. Cover tightly and simmer over very low heat for about 1 hour, or cook in the oven at 160°C, 325°F, Gas mark 3 for 1–1½ hours.

At the end of cooking time, uncover, stir well and taste. The bacon and sausage should have given enough salt to the sauce. Serve with plain boiled rice.

Quail with Almond Sauce and Saffron Dumplings

20g (¾oz) butter
4 quail, trussed for roasting
250ml (9fl oz) strong game stock
a blade of mace
2cm (¾in) piece of cinnamon stick
pinch of saffron threads
1 dessertspoon boiling water
60g (2¼oz) fresh breadcrumbs
30g (1oz) butter
1 egg yolk
60g (2¼oz) blanched almonds

120ml (4fl oz) single cream
1–2 teaspoons sugar
salt and black pepper

To garnish (optional)
30g (1oz) blanched pistachio nuts
the seeds from ½ large pomegranate
a few green or red grapes, halved
artichoke hearts, cut into slivers
asparagus spears

Melt the butter in a flameproof casserole just large enough to hold the birds. Fry them quickly until lightly browned. Discard the fat. Add the stock, mace, cinnamon and ¼ teaspoon salt. Simmer the birds gently for 25 minutes, until just cooked.

While they cook, soak the saffron in the water for about 10 minutes. Process it and the soaking liquid with the breadcrumbs and butter, plus some of the egg yolk (you'll probably need only about half). Shape into 20 very small dumplings. Add these to the broth in which the quail are stewing about 5 minutes before the end of cooking time. Remove and discard the cinnamon and mace.

When the birds are cooked, remove them and the little dumplings to a warm serving dish. Put the almonds and cream in a blender and whizz together until the almonds are pulverised. Pour this mixture into the cooking liquid and bring to the boil. Cook gently for a few minutes – it will foam up, so keep an eye on it. Add about 1 teaspoon sugar, taste and adjust the seasoning – neither sweet not salt should predominate. Pour around the birds and garnish as elaborately as desired with pistachio nuts and pomegranate seeds plus anything else from the list.

Roast Quail with
Vine Leaves and Grapes

In the United Kingdom, quail are almost always farmed, and generally very small. They are best quite plainly cooked, and the standard instruction in English cookery books of previous centuries was always to wrap them in vine leaves. This is a nice conceit, if you can beg or steal some fresh leaves from someone, although I'm not convinced it makes a great difference to the flavour.

serves
4

8 quail

a handful of small white seedless
   grapes

8 large vine leaves, if available

8 rashers unsmoked fat bacon, thinly
   cut, or unsmoked pancetta

unsalted butter, melted

100ml (3½fl oz) white wine

salt and pepper

Preheat the oven to 200°C, 400°F, Gas mark 6.

Season each bird with salt and pepper and pop a couple of grapes inside. Fold each bird in a vine leaf, then wrap a piece of bacon around it and tie in place with string. Brush each one with a little melted butter. Arrange the quail in a shallow roasting tin and pour over the white wine. Roast for 20–25 minutes, basting a couple of times with the wine and buttery juices.

Serve the quail still wrapped in their vine-leaf parcels, with the cooking juices, skimmed of fat. Game Chips (see page 170) go well with quail, and a green salad tastes better with quail than cooked vegetables.

Partridge with Cabbage

Partridges are usually treated with great respect in the English culinary tradition. Roasting was the favoured method for cooking, though it was admitted in cookery books that older birds needed stewing. The combination of partridges with cabbage, a classic of the French kitchen and good for using up birds past their youth, was noted by various writers in the early to mid-20th century. This is a variation on the theme.

serves 4

1 cabbage, preferably a pointed one, or January King
4 partridges
4 generous slices Parma ham
20g (¾oz) butter
1 medium onion, peeled and finely chopped
1 large garlic clove, peeled and crushed
2–3 juniper berries
200ml (7fl oz) white wine

a bouquet garni of a strip of lemon peel, a piece of celery, 1 sprig rosemary, 1 sprig thyme and a few stems of parsley, wrapped in a couple of green leaves from a leek
200ml (7fl oz) stock, preferably made with bones from game birds
30g (1oz) butter and 30g (1oz) flour, kneaded together
salt and black pepper

Discard any damaged leaves from the cabbage, then carefully detach 8–12 of the largest leaves from the outside. Keep them whole and put into a large pan. Bring a kettle of water to the boil, pour over the cabbage and boil for about 4 minutes. Pour into a colander and allow the leaves to drain well. Season each bird lightly with salt and pepper, then wrap in a slice of ham. Swaddle each bird up in two or three of the cabbage leaves.

Heat the butter in a flameproof casserole that will just hold the birds in one layer. Fry the onion gently until transparent, then add the garlic and juniper berries. Pour in the wine and bring it to the boil. Add the wrapped-up partridges, the bouquet garni, and the stock. Cover with buttered greaseproof paper, and then the lid of the casserole. Transfer to a low oven, 150°C, 300°F, Gas mark 2, and cook for about 1 hour (or 1½ hours if the partridges are older birds).

Remove the birds to a warm serving plate. Put the casserole with the cooking liquid over low heat and add the butter and flour mixture in small pieces. Stir and heat gently until the sauce thickens. Taste and correct the seasoning.

Partridge with Juniper Berries

Juniper berries were apparently not much liked in 18th-century England, if Martha Bradley (1756) is to be believed; she comments on how strange the flavour of them was to palates unaccustomed to them, and recommends that they be soaked in boiling water before use – presumably to take away some of their bitterness. I've increased their impact by adding a little gin to the recipe as well. A small glass of white wine can be used instead if you prefer.

serves 4

4 partridges, trussed
   for roasting
4 rashers unsmoked bacon
20g (¾oz) butter
2 tablespoons gin
200ml (7fl oz) strong beef stock

8–10 juniper berries
a little lemon juice
10g (¼oz) butter kneaded with
   10g (¼oz) flour
lemon slices, to garnish
salt

Cover the breasts of the birds with bacon and tie it on with thin string. Melt the butter in a flameproof casserole or small sauté pan. Brown the birds all over, then discard any fat from the pan. Warm the gin in a ladle, set light to it and pour it flaming over the birds. Add the beef stock and juniper berries, cover and simmer very gently for about 45 minutes. Turn the birds in the cooking liquid occasionally. At the end of cooking time they should be just cooked through; test the thickest part of the legs and cook a little longer if necessary.

Remove the birds from the cooking liquid and keep warm. Strain the juices into a clean pan and add a squeeze of lemon juice. Taste and add salt if necessary. Distribute the butter and flour mixture over the surface of the liquid, shaking the pan so that it is absorbed. Heat gently until it just comes to the boil and the sauce thickens slightly. Pour round the birds and serve garnished with slices of lemon.

Game

RABBITS ARE NOT NATIVE TO THE BRITISH ISLES, which is surprising considering how they breed in our countryside. Formerly they were considered a delicacy, carefully nurtured in warrens; then they escaped and became pests. In the 19th century, they were the only wild meat available to the rural poor, although taking them was sometimes regarded as poaching.

Venison once meant the flesh of any wild mammal hunted for food but has now come to apply specifically to the meat of deer. The right to hunt these animals was a jealously guarded privilege of the aristocracy in the past, and few ordinary people tasted the meat, unless it was poached. Deer prefer woodland habitats generally, but red deer, the largest, are now mostly found in the Scottish Highlands. Roe deer are found in woodland all over Britain. Fallow deer, also widespread, are probably a species introduced in the distant past, but seem to have been firmly established by the time of the Norman Conquest. All were much valued for meat by our ancestors. Venison was a mark of status, and there were many attempts to imitate it by marinating beef and mutton. The meat tends to dryness, and the real thing was often larded, wrapped in paper and enclosed in a coarse pastry of plain flour and water, sometimes with beef suet – before putting it to roast in front of an open fire.

Preparing rabbit

Rabbit was noted for its leanness and dryness, and in the past was usually larded. The heads were left on (but skinned) for roasting. The body cavities were sometimes lined with streaky bacon before cooking. Most rabbits sold in Britain are wild and their roasting qualities are uncertain. Active lives can be reflected in lean, dry meat and an excessively rabbity flavour. Treat them gently: marinades are useful for counteracting dryness and adding flavour; stuffing or barding also adds fat and flavour. They need to be well cooked. Wild rabbits weigh from 500g (1lb 2oz) to 1kg (2¼ lb); the heavier ones will feed 4 people. Most of the meat is in the hind legs and saddle, as the forequarter contains too much bone to be rewarding. They usually arrive skinned and paunched but should still contain the 'pluck' – the kidneys, liver, lungs and heart. Discard the lungs. The liver and kidneys are delicacies, and can be incorporated into a stuffing mixture or used to make stock or sauce.

Carving rabbit and accompaniments

The best meat in both hares and rabbits is in the saddle, the muscles lying on either side of and parallel to the backbone. Carve this in long, thin slices. Smaller slices can be cut from the hind legs. The shoulders, which according to Eliza Acton 'are not much esteemed though sometimes liked by sportsmen', should be taken off by dividing the joint from the ribs. Redcurrant jelly or other fruit jellies, such as quince or rowanberry, make excellent accompaniments for rabbit.

Buying, preparing and cooking venison

Farmed red deer venison is sold through supermarkets, butchers and by direct marketing. For wild venison, try a specialist game dealer. Red deer venison should be hung for 2 weeks. Wild red deer venison will be leaner and less predictable in quality but should be excellent. Venison generally is a dark-red, fine-grained meat, which is very lean and low in saturated fat.

Cuts for roasting are the same from all deer but vary greatly in size according to species. Those from red deer are largest; a saddle will be too large for many domestic ovens and is usually split down the backbone and divided into loin and best end. Saddles from smaller species are left whole. The haunch (hind leg) is also a prime cut. These joints are best slightly underdone. Shoulder makes a good slow roast or pot roast. Marinating, often recommended for venison, may have become popular because it acted as a short-term preservation method in the past. Whether to use a marinade or not is up to you. Venison has the potential to be extremely dry when roasted: larding repays the effort.

Carving venison and accompaniments

Carving the meat from the smaller species is similar to carving mutton or lamb, although saddle or loin of red deer should be carved like sirloin. Cookery authors in the past were very insistent that venison shouldn't be allowed to get cold, and must be served on very hot plates. French beans were considered the best vegetable to go with it. Redcurrant jelly is a traditional accompaniment for roast venison, but other fruit jellies, such as gooseberry, quince or sloe, go well too.

Cooking rabbit and venison in stews and pies

Both meats asre lean and share a tendency to be dry when cooked. Stewing is a good method, especially for meat from the forequarters. It keeps the meat moist, makes it tender. Most rabbit in Britain comes from wild animals: expect four portions from one rabbit. They are easy to joint and their flavour is improved by 1 hour's soaking in tepid water. When stewed slowly, they take less than 2 hours to cook. Light herby or aniseed flavours such as thyme or tarragon go well with them.

Like rabbit, venison benefits from long, slow stewing, especially the meat from the shoulder joints. Wine-rich stews made on the ragoos and braises of the past are excellent methods of cooking the meat (see Venison a la Bourguignonne, page 198). Any cooking method that is good for beef will also work with this meat, including fillings for pies. Rabbit and vemison stews are relatively good-tempered and reheat well; a boned rolled shoulder of venison is an exception to this rule, the meat becoming dry and any gelatinous bits setting to gristle. Stews made with smaller pieces of venison don't seem to suffer from this phenomenon and the flavour actually improves on reheating

Game Casserole

400–500g (14oz–1lb 2oz) meat cut
from game birds and animals
as available

2 tablespoons duck or goose fat, beef
dripping or lard

1 medium onion, peeled and chopped

1 celery stick, chopped

1 medium carrot, trimmed, peeled
and chopped

2 garlic cloves, peeled and crushed

1 teaspoon ground coriander

a bouquet garni of 1 bay leaf, thyme,
marjoram, parsley and a few strips
of orange zest

200ml (7fl oz) red wine

10g (¼oz) dried porcini

200ml (7fl oz) boiling water

50g (2oz) bacon or pancetta, cut
into small dice

1 tablespoon balsamic vinegar
(optional)

salt and black pepper

Cut the meat as neatly as possible into 2cm (¾in) cubes. Heat the fat in a frying pan and add the onion, celery and carrot. Fry briskly, turning often, until they begin to turn slightly golden. Add the garlic, coriander and bouquet garni and pour in the wine. Simmer gently for 10–15 minutes, making sure that not too much liquid evaporates. Pour everything into a large bowl and allow to cool, then add the meat. Turn well in the mixture, cover and leave in a cold place overnight.

Next day, wash the porcini and put them in a small bowl. Pour over the boiling water and leave for at least 30 minutes to infuse.

Tip the meat into a strainer over a bowl. Keep the marinade that drips through, and the bouquet garni. Heat a flameproof casserole and fry the bacon or pancetta until it has yielded most of its fat. Remove the pieces and keep to one side. Blot any excess liquid off the meat, then fry it in the bacon fat. When the pieces are browned, remove from pan. Pour in the reserved marinade and bring to the boil, strain and return to the pan. Add the bouquet garni, the porcini and their soaking liquid, all the meat, and salt and pepper to taste, then return to a simmer.

Cover with greaseproof paper or foil and then the lid of the casserole. Cook in a low oven, 150°C, 300°F, Gas mark 2, for about 1½ hours, or until the meat is cooked. Stir in the vinegar at the end, if using. Good with jacket potatoes and a dish of cabbage cooked with juniper berries.

Roast Rabbit with Apple

Rabbit responds well to the apple and cream treatment more usually associated with pheasant.

serves
4

3–4 tablespoons Calvados or whisky
1–2 tablespoons cider vinegar
the leaves from a few fresh thyme
   sprigs
4–5 juniper berries, crushed
1 rabbit

1–2 aromatic dessert apples
bacon fat, butter or olive oil
   for barding, optional
150ml (5fl oz) double cream
salt and pepper

Mix the Calvados or whisky, cider vinegar, thyme and juniper berries in a deep glass or china bowl. Add the rabbit and let it marinate for 2–3 hours.

Preheat the oven to 150°C, 300°F, Gas mark 2.

When ready to cook, peel and core the apples and cut them into small chunks. Take the rabbit out of the marinade and stuff the body cavity with the apples. Grease the roasting tin and put the rabbit in (bard the meat if desired, although this is not strictly necessary). Add the marinade, and cover with foil. Roast gently for about 1–1½ hours; check to make sure the juices don't catch, and add a little water or light stock if necessary.

When the rabbit is cooked, remove it to a warmed serving dish. There should be a small amount of concentrated juice left in the roasting tin (boil to reduce it to a few syrupy tablespoons if it seems on the liquid side). Add the cream and bring back to the boil; the sauce should be quite thick. Taste and adjust the seasoning.

Rabbit with Cider and Dumplings

serves
4

1 rabbit, jointed
brine, optional

For the marinade
400ml (14fl oz) cider
zest of 1 lemon, finely grated
2 garlic cloves, chopped
8 juniper berries, bruised
a bouquet garni of several
    sprigs parsley and thyme
    and 2 sprigs rosemary

For the stew
100g (3½oz) bacon, cut into lardons
about 30g (1oz) butter
1 medium onion, finely chopped
about 30g (1oz) flour
salt and black pepper

For the dumplings
1 quantity dumpling mixture
    (see page 26)
1 tablespoon chopped parsley
leaves from 2–3 sprigs thyme, chopped

Put the rabbit in a bowl and pour over the brine, if using. Leave in a cool place for a few hours, then drain, discarding the brine. Rinse the bowl and replace the pieces of rabbit. Mix the marinade ingredients, pepper thoroughly and pour over the rabbit joints. Cover and leave overnight.

When ready to cook the stew, drain the rabbit and reserve the marinade. Add the bacon to large frying pan and let it cook gently until all the fat has run out. Remove the bacon to a dish. Add the butter and fry the onion fairly briskly until it is translucent. Remove with a slotted spoon, allowing as much fat as possible to run back into the pan or casserole. Put the onion with the bacon.

Pat the rabbit joints dry, dredge with flour and fry them in the remaining fat until lightly browned. Dust in any remaining flour and pour in the marinade. Add the bacon and onions, stirring well, plus ½ teaspoon salt and a generous amount of black pepper. Transfer the pan contents to a casserole. Cover, put in the oven and cook at 140°C, 275°F, Gas mark 1 for 1½ hours.

Make up the dumpling mixture, incorporating the herbs, and use a spoon to drop pieces the size of a large walnut on to the top of the stew. Return to the oven for a further 20 minutes. Finally, turn the oven up to 180°C, 350°F, Gas mark 4 and cook for another 10 minutes to help the dumplings cook through.

Venison and Mushroom Pie

This recipe is adapted from the robust pub-lunch tradition. The pie is more usually made with beef (which works equally in this recipe), but it is a good way of using stewing venison.

serves
4

1 medium onion, peeled
60g (2¼oz) lard, beef dripping
    or light oil such as sunflower oil
2 garlic cloves, peeled
leaves from 2 sprigs rosemary
250g (9oz) button mushrooms,
    trimmed and sliced
500g (1lb 2oz) stewing venison,
    cubed

30g (1oz) flour, plus extra for dusting
150ml (5fl oz) red wine
about 300ml (10fl oz) game
    or beef stock
1 tablespoon chopped parsley
leaves from 4–5 sprigs thyme
1 quantity puff pastry (see page 25)
beaten egg, cream or milk, to glaze
salt and black pepper

Chop the onion fairly finely. Heat half the fat or oil in a large frying pan and add the onion. Let it cook quite briskly, stirring frequently. Chop the garlic and rosemary leaves small and add them to the onion. Keep frying and stirring until the onion are just beginning to go brown. Remove from the pan with a slotted spoon and put in a casserole.

Fry the mushrooms in the fat remaining in the pan. Keep the heat quite high so that any juice they exude evaporates. When they have browned a little add to the onion mixture.

Toss the venison in flour. Add the remaining fat to the frying pan if necessary and brown the venison in batches, transferring it to the casserole when done. Dust any remaining flour into the frying pan and stir to absorb any residual fat. Pour in the wine and keep stirring, scraping up the residues from the base of the pan. Add two-thirds of the stock and bring to the boil, stirring constantly. Add the chopped parsley, thyme, 1 teaspoon salt and some black pepper. Pour over the meat and onions in the casserole. Stir, cover tightly and transfer to a low oven, 140°C, 275°F, Gas mark 1, for 2½ –3 hours. Check occasionally and stir in the remaining stock if the mixture seems dry.

At the end of this time, the meat should be tender. Skim off any excess fat, taste and correct the seasoning. Pour into a deep pie dish.

Dust a work surface with flour and roll out the pastry. Cover the dish (see page 24), decorating the pie as desired. Brush with egg wash, cream or milk.

Bake at 220°C, 425°F, Gas mark 7 for 15 minutes to raise and set the pastry, then reduce the heat to 180°C, 350°F, Gas mark 4 and then cook for another 30 minutes, until the filling is thoroughly hot.

Venison à la Bourguignonne

Meaty stews of this type with red wine, mushrooms and onions, crept into English cookery after the Second World War. The recipe was originally intended for beef, but works well with venison. The sauce of red wine enriched with bacon, mushrooms and little onions recalls the rich ragoos of 18th-century, French-influenced cookery.

serves 4

500g (1lb 2oz) stewing venison, cut into slices about half the size of a postcard and 5mm (¼in) thick
1 medium onion, peeled and sliced
1 garlic clove, peeled and crushed
4 juniper berries, bruised
75ml (2½fl oz) red wine
1 tablespoon olive oil
about 40g (1½oz) butter or beef dripping
2 rashers bacon, cut into strips

8–10 tiny onions, peeled
120g (4oz) button mushrooms, trimmed and sliced
20g (¾oz) flour
175ml (6fl oz) beef stock
a bouquet garni of parsley, thyme, marjoram, a bay leaf and a strip of orange peel
salt and black pepper

Put the venison, onion, garlic, juniper berries, wine and olive oil in a bowl. Add 1 scant teaspoon salt and a generous grind of pepper. Cover and leave to marinate overnight.

The next day, tip the meat into a sieve over a bowl and allow to drain, reserving the marinade. Melt half the butter or dripping in a heavy casserole and add the bacon. Cook gently and remove when it shows signs of crisping. Add the little onions and fry them, turning often, until they start to develop golden patches. Remove them and add to the bacon. Cook the mushrooms in the same fat until soft. Lift out with a slotted spoon and put aside with the bacon and onions.

Toss the drained meat (don't worry too much about disentangling the onion) with the flour. Add more butter or dripping to the pan if necessary and brown the pieces. Then pour in the marinade, stirring well. Gradually add the stock, stirring while the mixture comes to the boil.

Put the bouquet garni in among the meat, cover, and transfer to a low oven, 140–150°C, 275–300°F, Gas mark 1–2, for about 3 hours. Towards the end of cooking, stir in the bacon, mushrooms and onions. Taste and correct the seasoning as necessary.

Serve with jacket potatoes, mashed potato or pappardelle, tossed with a little butter and some chopped parsley.

Fish

ENGLISH COOKERY SEEMED TO FORGET THE IDEA of stewing fish sometime during the 19th century. Poaching, yes; stewing, not really but were the two ideas the same? Previous generations blithely plunged all sorts of fish into hot water, with or without added seasonings, and then called the results a stew. Perhaps the change was more apparent than real, and linked to the usage of words. Recipes from the 17th century indicate that stewing often meant simple, fast cooking in water. The idea of the court-bouillon – a mixture of water, wine and herbs – made its way into English cookery from French, probably in the mid- to late 17th century. This was swiftly followed by increasing elaboration, as fish stews followed the trend in the 18th century towards complicated dishes with luxurious ragoos and garnishes. The habit of adding meaty stocks to these seems especially strange to us. A trend back to simplicity returned in the 19th century and lasted until after the Second World War.

Our ancestors who lived near the coast, or perhaps on an inland port on an estuary, enjoyed an extraordinary variety of locally available fish – including soles, turbot and lobster. Salmon was commonplace, caught from wild populations migrating up rivers to spawn. Oysters, which were then cheap and plentiful, were routinely added to savoury dishes of all kinds; mussels took a distant second place to these.

Another major difference lay in the sheer variety of fish that cooks were expected to handle. Eels, carp, perch, pike, tench, trout and crayfish all appear to have been common; sturgeon and lampreys were not unknown. The range of freshwater fish, in particular, is startling to us today. Rivers were relatively unpolluted; the ornamental lakes of landscaped gardens, such as those of Fountains Abbey and Studley Royal, were stocked for recreational fishing; and artificial fishponds provided fresh fish far from the sea. Some people still observed the Catholic habit of abstaining from meat on Fridays and during Lent.

Our range has shrunk. True, many freshwater fish have to be very fresh to taste good, and can be prone to muddy flavours, or an excess of little bones, but our kitchens are poorer without them. Fish routinely available in the past are impossible to buy. Eels, whose fatty flesh made them useful for larding other, leaner fish are difficult to obtain, while oysters, once ubiquitous, are now expensive and therefore less often used.

Dishes such as a fish pie composed of layers of lobster flesh, breadcrumbs and oysters, finished with a mixture of gravy and cream – a recipe given by Dr A. Hunter in 1807 – sound utterly delicious but remain in the world of fantasy. Maybe they always were.

Cooking fish stews and pies

Because of the fragile nature of fish, stews made with them run counter to the general rules of long cooking. Depending on the size of the fish, they will take 10–20 minutes to cook on even the gentlest simmer. Don't try to keep them warm for any length of time and avoid reheating, which will make the fish dry. Nor do fish stews begin with the basic operation of frying, in the way that meat ones do. White fish are generally best for stews; stocks are now overfished, so it is best to take advice on individual species – the National Trust follows Marine Stewardship Council advice (see www.mac.org). Both salmon and trout are readily available from fish farms.

Plain water can be used for stewing fish or for fish stocks and broths, as it was in the past. Replacing part of it with an ingredient such as white wine, lemon juice, verjuice or even cider often gives a better flavour, unless the fish is straight out of a lake. 20–30 minutes is long enough to make a simple fish stock for the recipes given here. Good herbs for flavouring and garnishing fish stews include parsley, chives, lemon thyme, chervil, fennel, dill and tarragon.

Stewed fish dishes in the past were often thickened with flour and butter added at the last minute, or with a roux. Using potato to give body to a fish stew never seems to have made its way into upper-class English cookery, nor does adding cream to enrich a simple stock. Both occur in the British-influenced cookery of New England; this may have derived from the food of other countries, or of the rural poor in Britain, whose traditions have been so inadequately recorded. Both are excellent additions. Potatoes may hold their shape or dissolve partially or completely into the liquid, giving a pleasing texture.

Adding shellfish such as oysters to a fish about 5 minutes before the end of cooking time – just enough to cook them through but not to toughen them – would have won our ancestors' approval. Diced ham or lean bacon is also good with fish – try cooking some lightly at the start and adding it to the cooking liquid, or crisping small pieces of bacon to garnish fish stews.

To Stew Soles

This recipe is based on one that appears in an early Scottish cookery book by Elizabeth Cleland: *A New and Easy Method of Cookery* (1755). A simple method for cooking soles or any other flat fish, it needs a wide shallow pan in which they will fit in one layer. Ask the fishmonger to remove the skins from the soles.

**serves
2**

2 small soles, each weighing about
   250g (9oz)
120ml (4fl oz) white wine
a few peppercorns
1 blade of mace
a strip of lemon zest about
   3cm (1¼in) long
100g (3½oz) shelled prawns (optional)

1 generous teaspoon butter
1 generous teaspoon flour
salt

To serve
finely chopped parsley
lemon wedges

Put the soles side by side in a shallow pan and pour the wine over. Add the peppercorns, mace and lemon zest, and a good pinch of salt. Bring to a simmer, then cover (use foil if the pan doesn't have a lid) and cook over a low heat for 10 minutes. At the end of this time, the fish should be cooked through, although the upper side might not be quite done – the best way to deal with this is to put the pan under a hot grill for 2–3 minutes. Add a little water if the cooking liquid shows signs of evaporating – there should be about the same amount as at the start.

When the soles are cooked, remove them to warmed plates. Put the pan with the cooking liquid back over low heat. Remove the spices and lemon zest and add the prawns, if using. Allow them to heat through to boiling. Knead the flour and butter together and dot over the surface of the liquid, shaking the pan so that it disperses and thickens the sauce. Stir and pour over the fish.

Sprinkle with parsley, and garnish with lemon wedges.

Fish Pie

800–900g (1lb 12oz–2lb) floury
potatoes, peeled and cut into
chunks
30g (1oz) butter
50ml (2fl oz) milk
50–60g (2–2¼oz) coarsely grated
cheese – Gruyère for a mild flavour,
or strong Cheddar for something
more English
600g (1lb 5oz) cod or haddock fillet
250g (9oz) shell-on prawns

For making stock
the skin and any bones from the fish
the shells from the prawns
150ml (5fl oz) white wine

2 celery sticks, washed and cut into
1cm (½in) lengths
about 6cm (2½in) of the green leaves
from a leek, washed and cut into
thick slices
a few sprigs parsley
a small carrot, scrubbed and cut
into quarters
750ml (1¼ pints) water

For the sauce
30g (1oz) butter
30g (1oz) flour
75g (3oz) creme fraîche
salt and black pepper

Put all the ingredients for the stock into a pan, bring to the boil and simmer for
25–30 minutes. Strain, discarding the debris.

To make the sauce, melt the butter in a clean pan, stir in the flour and cook for
a moment without browning. Stir in about 300ml (10fl oz) fish stock to make a
smooth sauce. Allow to cook gently for 5–10 minutes, adding a little more stock
if it seems too thick (the remaining stock can be frozen if you have no immediate
use for it). Add the creme fraîche and season with salt and pepper to taste.

In the meantime, boil the potatoes until tender, drain and mash with the butter,
milk and cheese. Season with salt and pepper to taste.

Cut the fish fillets into neat slices about 2cm (¾in) wide and arrange them in the
bottom of a deep ovenproof dish. Scatter the peeled prawns over the top. Pour in
the sauce and top with the mashed potato. Use a fork to roughen the surface.

Bake at 190°C, 375°F, Gas mark 5 for 30–40 minutes until golden brown.

Cullen Skink

This is a version of a traditional Scottish soup of smoked fish and potatoes. I've altered it very slightly to push it closer to North American chowder-type dishes, and give something in between a soup and a stew. It makes a good light lunch or supper.

serves
4

400–500g (14oz–1lb 2oz)
   smoked haddock
1 small onion, peeled and sliced
a bay leaf
a few peppercorns

700g (1lb 8oz) floury potatoes, peeled
   and cut into 1cm (½in) cubes
100ml (3½fl oz) single cream
salt
chopped chives or 2 spring onions,
   very finely sliced, to garnish

Put the smoked haddock, sliced onion, bay leaf and peppercorns into a pan and cover with water. Heat and allow to simmer for about 10 minutes or until the fish is cooked. Remove it from the pan (keep the cooking liquid). When the fish has cooled enough to handle, remove all the skin and bones. Flake the flesh and set on one side. Return the bones and skin to the pan, cover and simmer for about 30 minutes longer to make a stock. Strain and measure it – you will need about 600–700ml (1–1¼ pints). If there isn't enough, make up the quantity with water.

Put the stock and the potatoes into a clean pan and bring to the boil. Let them simmer until the potatoes are well cooked and just starting to break up a little, giving body to the liquid. Stir in the fish and heat through. Taste and add more salt if desired; remember, the smoked fish may be quite salty. Stir in the cream.

Divide between 4 soup bowls and scatter each portion with chopped chives or a little spring onion. Serve with wholemeal bread.

Trout Pie

The 18th-century recipe that inspired this idea, required 6 trout, each weighing about 900g (2lb). I've added some contemporary south-east Asian flavours, adapting to changing tastes and available ingredients just as people did in the past.

serves 4–6

6 trout, each weighing approximately 300g (11oz)

½ teaspoon salt

1 tablespoon each of chopped fresh coriander, basil, chives

300ml (10fl oz) strong fish stock

1 tablespoon fresh root ginger matchsticks

2 kaffir lime leaves

2cm (¾in) lemongrass, thinly sliced

1 hot red chilli, seeds removed, thinly sliced

150–200g (5–7oz) uncooked king prawns, peeled

For the pie crust

a little butter, for greasing

flour, for dusting

1 quantity puff pastry (see page 25)

beaten egg, cream or milk, for glazing

Remove the heads and tails of the trout and fillet them. Trim off any fins and wipe the fish well. Reserve the 4 largest ones. Skin the other two and blend them with the salt to a paste in a food processor. Stir in the chopped herbs. Divide this mixture between the four whole fish, folding them over to enclose the stuffing.

To make the pie crust, take a deep pie dish and butter it well. Lay the stuffed trout in it. Dust the work surface with flour and roll the pastry out to about 5mm (¼in) thick, then cover the dish (see page 24). Brush the pastry with beaten egg, cream or milk. Bake in a hot oven, 220°C, 425°F, Gas mark 7, for 15 minutes to rise and set the pastry, then reduce the heat to 180°C, 350°F, Gas mark 4 and cook for another 15 minutes. Remove from the oven.

Heat the fish stock in a pan with the ginger, lime leaves, lemongrass and chilli. When it comes to the boil add the prawns. Simmer for 3–4 minutes until the prawns are cooked through – stir occasionally so that they cook evenly.

Cut through the edge of the pastry and lift it off. Pour the prawn mixture on top of the trout. Cut the pastry into neat wedges and then use to garnish the pie. Serve hot with a green vegetable accompaniment.

Haddock, Leek and Potato Stew with Mussels

This dish is recorded on the eastern seaboard of the Atlantic, where lobscouse, which is traditional to the north-western coast of England and some ports in Germany and Scandinavia, was sometimes made with salt fish. Chowder, as made on the New England coast of the USA, is a related dish. Onions were the usual vegetable, but leeks also give a good flavour and pretty contrast of colour. Ask the fishmonger to skin the fish, but get him to put the skin in the parcel, together with some fish bones if possible.

serves
4

500–600g (1lb 2oz–1lb 5oz) haddock, skins and bones removed and reserved
a few stalks or leaves of parsley
1 celery stalk
2 leeks, washed, trimmed and cut into 2cm (¾in) slices (keep the trimmings)

about 600ml (1 pint) water
300g (11oz) mussels
2 large potatoes, peeled and cut into 1cm (½in) dice
60ml (2fl oz) single cream
a little fresh tarragon, chopped (optional)
salt and black pepper

Simmer the fish skin, bones, parsley, celery and trimmings of leek in a pan with the water gently for 20 minutes, then strain, reserving the liquid as stock.

Pull the beards off the mussels, discarding any that don't close when tapped. Put them in a pan with a tight-fitting lid and steam over fairly high heat for a few minutes. Strain the liquor into the fish stock, and keep the mussels on one side.

Put the potatoes and leeks into a pan or a flameproof casserole. Pour over the stock and season with 1 scant teaspoon salt and a little pepper. Cook for about 10 minutes, until the potatoes are just tender. Cut the haddock into slices about 2cm (¾in) thick, and put them on the top of the vegetables. Simmer for another 5 minutes, or until the fish is just done. Add the mussels and heat through.

Put the vegetables and fish into soup bowls and pour the cooking liquid over. Add a spoonful of cream to each portion and scatter with chopped tarragon.

Vegetables

THE ENGLISH DIET IS RESOLUTELY MEATY, and vegetables play a secondary role. Sometimes they are used as a support to the main ingredient (as in the use of asparagus and artichokes as garnishes), and sometimes they appear simply as extras, in which case they were often boiled in water. Boiling, in this case, is most emphatically not stewing. For those people who were very poor, a small amount of meat, sometimes just a few pieces of bacon, added savour to pots of cabbage, dried beans or peas, or potatoes. Little of this is recorded, so we don't know to what extent these may have included dishes that had the potential to become social climbers, like the cassoulets of south-west France. The remnants of dried-pulse dishes that survived – black peas in south-west Lancashire, mushy peas – were reduced to the most basic of poverty foods, and dried pea and bean dishes from the Indian subcontinent failed to transplant when East India Company employees returned to Britain with the notion of curry in the 18th century.

Yet the British country-house tradition included huge walled kitchen gardens and some of the best gardeners in the world, skilled in growing all kinds of crops and producing out-of-season delicacies for the kitchen. From artichokes to watercress, the most delicate of spring sea kale to the largest of winter turnips, a regular sequence of vegetables was available to the landed gentry by the 18th century, and to a lesser extent to those who shopped in metropolitan markets supplied by market gardeners on the fringes of towns.

Many vegetables must have ended up in boiling water, but the 18th-century fashion for complicated food produced other dishes. Some were popular as ingredients for fricassées, notably mushrooms and various root vegetables such as parsnips; this idea hung over into the post-war period in the form of carrots served in white sauce. Green peas *à la française* became fashionable, too, and many vegetables were put into ragoos, including onions, mushrooms and celery, cooked with strong meat stocks.

Delicacies like artichoke hearts were used in 17th-century pie fillings, as one item among many, and carrots or potatoes were cooked, mashed and mixed with sugar for sweet pie fillings. In the early 19th century, Mrs Rundell suggested a pie filling of broad beans, young carrots, turnips, mushrooms, peas, onions, lettuce, parsley, celery 'or any of them that you have' stewed in veal gravy and served under a ready-baked pie crust – very different to the vegetable pies of mid-20th century war-time rationing.

Cooking vegetable stews and pies

Vegetables vary enormously in flavour and texture and it is difficult to formulate rules about stew-type dishes made from them. On the whole, it is better not to overcook them, but some respond well to long, slow simmering, which enhances their sweetness and allows the flavours to mellow, or helps to break down tough fibres (members of the cabbage family, however, are best cooked quickly).

Think, instead, in terms of the end product. For a fricassée, cook the vegetables until they are just done: the result should be light and fresh, and the flavours will not be improved by overcooking. Most vegetables respond well to this, the main point being to adjust the cooking times – short for spring and summer asparagus or beans, longer for winter roots. The light, slightly acid sauce of a fricassée means it doesn't need meat stock to make it interesting.

In ragoos and braised dishes a strong stock, preferably a jellied beef one, is essential to the true nature of the dish. Starting the vegetables off in a little butter, followed by long slow cooking, helps to mellow the flavour and evaporate the liquid, so that at the end just a little highly flavoured glaze remains to coat them. This is a particularly good method for celery and winter root vegetables, and small pieces of bacon make good additions.

The idea of stewing vegetables in olive oil is not traditional to English cookery, but took root sometime in the late 1950s or early 1960s, when ratatouille became a popular dish. The idea is not specific to this dish, though – you can also use it for onions or courgettes cooked together or alone. It is also a good cooking method for combinations of summer vegetables (see Sarah's Summer Vegetable Stew, page 213), but take care not to overcook them.

Cooking pulses

Pulses – lentils, dried peas and beans – can be used with or without meat. Lentils and dried split peas can be cooked without soaking, but dried beans need to be soaked overnight or for about 12 hours and then boiled rapidly for 10 minutes. After this, drain them, add fresh water and cook gently until tender. Don't add salt until the end of the cooking time. Nearly all pulse dishes now in the British cookery repertoire have been derived from France, Spain, Italy or Asia, mostly during the last 40 years.

Sarah's Summer Vegetable Stew

This recipe, given to me by a friend, makes the most of late spring and summer vegetables. It is essentially an easy-going mixture of the best from the garden or the market. The onion, asparagus, broad beans and peas are essential; make up the remaining weight with a selection of the other vegetables listed. Sarah suggests crusty bread and pesto as accompaniments.

serves 4

200g (7oz) asparagus, trimmed
100g (3½oz) broad beans
   (after podding)
100g (3½oz) peas (after podding)
500g (1lb 2oz) of other vegetables
   as available – choose from other
   bean varieties such as French,
   runner or bobby beans; mangetouts
   or sugar peas; small courgettes;
   Florentine fennel; and young,
   small globe artichokes
150ml (5fl oz) olive oil
1 large onion, chopped fairly finely

a bouquet garni of a bay leaf, thyme
   and parsley, plus summer savory
300ml (10fl oz) white wine
1 teaspoon salt

For the butterballs
60g (2¼oz) fresh breadcrumbs
30g (1oz) butter
1 egg yolk
pinch of salt
1 tablespoon chopped herbs
   to taste, e.g. parsley, chives,
   tarragon and chervil

Cut the asparagus into 2cm (¾in) lengths. Trim the beans, mangetouts or sugar peas and cut into 2cm (¾in) lengths as well. Trim the courgettes and cut into short lengths if very small, or dice 1–2cm (½ –¾in) square if larger. Trim the fennel, discarding any tough or blemished outer layers and cut into dice like the courgettes. Trim the stems and cut the tops off globe artichokes, then scoop out and discard the thistle-like choke from the centre. Cut them in quarters.

Heat the oil in a large flameproof casserole. Add the onion, bouquet garni and summer savory. Cook over a low heat until the onions turn translucent. Add the asparagus, broad beans, peas and other vegetables. Heat through, turning them in the oil. Add the wine and salt and cook gently, turning occasionally, until the vegetables are cooked through but not too soft. Taste and check the seasoning.

Make the butterballs: whizz all the ingredients in a blender and form into 20 little balls. Drop into the vegetable mixture and simmer for 5 minutes. Serve in bowls.

Peas with Cream

The idea of eating fresh green peas became fashionable sometime during the 17th century. They were often cooked with butter and herbs in the manner that we still know as *à la française*, but there were variations, such as adding cream. Serve with good bread for a light lunch or supper, or to accompany egg or cheese dishes, or plainly grilled meat or fish.

serves
4

2–4 lettuce hearts, depending on size; use Little Gem, Cos or cabbage lettuces
20g (¾oz) butter
250g (9oz) green peas (shelled weight)
2 tablespoons water
½ teaspoon salt
½ teaspoon sugar

pinch of nutmeg
1 teaspoon butter kneaded with 1 teaspoon flour (optional)
4 tablespoons double cream
a mixture of fresh chives, mint, chervil or tarragon – enough to make about 2 tablespoons when finely chopped

Remove any raggedy outer leaves from the lettuces. Cut them in half lengthways, wash them and then shake as dry as possible.

Put a frying pan over very gentle heat and melt the butter in it. Add the lettuces, cut side down. Put the peas in around them. Add the water, remembering that the lettuces will produce liquid as they cook. Sprinkle in the salt and sugar and grate in a little nutmeg.

Cover the pan closely (use foil if it doesn't have a lid) and cook, very gently, for 25 minutes. Check every few minutes at the start to make sure that it isn't drying up, and also towards the end to see how much juice the vegetables have yielded. If there seems to be more than a couple of tablespoonfuls, remove the cover of the pan for the last few minutes.

At the end of cooking time, remove the lettuce to a warmed serving dish (if there still seems to be a lot of juice in the pan with the peas, distribute the flour and butter mixture over the surface and heat gently, shaking the pan until the sauce thickens). Add the cream, stir well and heat until nearly boiling, then pour over the lettuce. Sprinkle with the chopped herbs and serve.

Root Vegetable Pie

The original of this recipe was Woolton Pie, which became infamous during the Second World War. It was a dish of root vegetables, such as swede and parsnip, cooked under an oatmeal pie crust – plain as plain could be and apparently much disliked by a nation desperate for meat and other luxuries. I thought it would be interesting to update it with more unusual vegetables.

serves
4

300g (11oz) Jerusalem artichokes
300g (11oz) celeriac
300g (11oz) leek (white part only)
300g (11oz) waxy potatoes (such as
    Anya, Pink Fir Apple)
120g (4oz) well-flavoured cheese –
    a good Cheddar, or try Blue Stilton,
    cut into thin slices or crumbled

40g (1½oz) butter
40g (1½oz) flour, plus a little extra
    for rolling the pastry
600ml (1 pint) milk
pinch of nutmeg
1 quantity puff pastry (see page 25)
beaten egg, cream or milk, to glaze
salt and black pepper

Wash the Jerusalem artichokes, put them in a pan, cover with water and simmer for 10–15 minutes, or until just tender. Drain and cover with cold water; once they are cool enough to handle, peel off the papery skin. Cut the flesh into julienne strips. Wash and peel the celeriac and cut into julienne strips. Wash the leek and slice thinly. Wash the potatoes, peel if desired and cut into julienne strips.

Put the artichokes into a deep dish, scatter over about a quarter of the cheese, and repeat with the other vegetables and remainder of the cheese.

Melt the butter in a pan, stir in the flour, then add the milk to make a sauce. Season with salt, pepper and a scrape of nutmeg. Pour this over the vegetables.

Use the extra flour to dust a work surface and roll out the pastry. Use it to cover the dish (see page 24), trimming nicely, and making decorative leaves as desired. Make a hole for steam to escape and brush with egg, cream or milk. Transfer to a hot oven, 220°C, 425°F, Gas mark 7, for 20 minutes, then turn the heat down to 180°C, 350°F, Gas mark 4 and cook for a further 40 minutes.

Butterbean Casserole

The idea of eating vegetable dishes that were actually vegetarian — no bits of bacon, no meat stock — was a novel one in the Britain of the late 19th century. The Food Reform Movement did their best within the conventions of the time, trying to work out substitutes for the vast amounts of protein seen as necessary for health. At the same time, things that would now be considered good additions, such as olive oil, garlic and herbs, weren't used either because of snobbish ideas about 'greasiness' and bad breath, or simply because they weren't obtainable. The butter bean stew made by my mother probably originated with ideas from this time and I have incorporated a few things either unavailable or frowned upon in earlier days.

serves
4

150g (5oz) dried butter beans
3–4 tablespoons olive oil
1 large onion, peeled and
    finely chopped
2 garlic cloves, peeled and
    finely chopped
leaves from 1 sprig rosemary,
    finely chopped
100ml (3½fl oz) white wine
a bouquet garni of a bay leaf, a few
    sprigs parsley and some thyme
about 350ml (12fl oz) water
400ml (14fl oz) passata
    (sieved tomato pulp)
a handful of basil leaves, chopped

For the topping
4 slices good white bread, crusts
    removed, cut into triangles
about 4 tablespoons good olive oil
about 40g (1½oz) strongly flavoured
    cheese, such as Pecorino Romano
    or a good Cheddar, finely grated
1–2 tablespoons pine nuts (optional)
salt and pepper

Soak the beans overnight in cold water. Next day, bring them and the water to the boil and cook rapidly for 10 minutes. Drain, discarding the water.

Heat about 3 tablespoons olive oil in a flameproof casserole. Add the onion, garlic and rosemary. Cook briskly, stirring often, until the onion begins to brown slightly. Lower the heat and add the beans, turning them in the mixture.

Add the wine, the bouquet garni and the water. Bring to the boil, cover, and then cook either on very low heat on the hob or in a moderate oven, 150°C, 300°F,

Gas mark 2, for about 1¼ hours, or until the beans are soft. Stir occasionally and check the liquid level. Add a little more water if they seem to be drying out. When they are fully softened, season with about ½ teaspoon salt and some black pepper. Turn the oven up to 200°C, 400°F, Gas mark 6. Add the passata in a layer on top of the beans and scatter the chopped basil over the top.

Dip the pieces of bread in olive oil (lightly, don't try to saturate them) and arrange over the top as if making bread-and-butter pudding. Sprinkle with grated cheese and scatter over the pine nuts (if using). Return the dish to the oven, uncovered, and allow the topping to brown and crisp for about 10 minutes; check from time to time to make sure that it doesn't scorch.

This is a filling dish and the best accompaniments are either a salad or some lightly cooked summer vegetables.

Chestnut and Shallot Pie

This recipe began as an attempt to make a vegetarian equivalent of my grandmother's meat and potato pie, a plain but comforting dish of the farmhouse and urban industrial communities in Yorkshire and Lancashire. Along the way, it developed into something much richer. If you are not concerned with being strictly vegetarian, add about 50g (2oz) pancetta cubes, well fried and drained of their fat, to the chestnut and shallot mixture.

 serves 4–6

30g (1oz) butter, plus extra for
   the potatoes
200g (7oz) shallots, peeled
8 garlic cloves, peeled
200g (7oz) cooked, peeled chestnuts
   (use vacuum packed ones)
2 tablespoons brandy
1 tablespoon chopped parsley
leaves from 1 sprig rosemary, chopped
leaves from 5–6 sprigs thyme

75ml (2½fl oz) single cream
2 tablespoons truffle paste (optional)
50ml (2fl oz) water
800g (1lb 12oz) potatoes, peeled
   and sliced
1 quantity puff pastry (see page 25)
flour, for dusting
beaten egg, cream or milk,
   for glazing
salt and black pepper

Melt the butter in a large frying pan. Add the shallots and fry gently until they begin to develop golden brown patches. Add the garlic and cook for a few moments longer. Add the chestnuts and pour in the brandy. Allow it to bubble, then stir in the herbs and cream. Add the truffle paste if using, plus the water. Taste and add salt and pepper as desired.

Put the mixture in a deep pie dish. Layer the sliced potatoes over the top, dotting a little butter between and sprinkling lightly with salt. Dust a work surface with flour and roll out the pastry to about 5mm (¼in) thick. Use this to cover the pie (see page 24), and decorate the top with pastry leaves if desired. Cut a hole for the steam to escape, and brush with beaten egg, cream or milk.

Start the pie off in a hot oven, 220°C, 425°F, Gas mark 7, for 20 minutes, then turn the heat down to 180°C, 350°F, Gas mark 4 and cook for 40 minutes or until the potatoes feel done when tested with a knife through the steam hole. A salad of peppery or bitter leaves such as watercress or rocket is good with this.

Index